Relatable God

Donna Robinson

2020 SheEO Publishing Company

RELATABLE GOD

Cover Artwork: Markapone, *L'autonomisation des Femmes,* Instagram: @marka_pone

Workmanship chapter illustration: Manasseh Johnson, Sr., *Creation of Man,* www.manassehart.com

Interior Design and Editing: SheEO Publishing

Published in the United States by SheEO Publishing, Atlanta, GA 30305 www.sheeopublishing.com

ISBN-13: 978-0-578-79920-9

ISBN-10: 978-0-578-79919-3

For general information or other products and services, contact Donna Robinson at relatablegodministries@gmail.com

Printed in the United States of America

ৰ্চ

To my Best Friend,
Who also happens to be the Savior
of the whole world. ;)

ৰ্চ

What People Are Saying About Relatable God

Relatable God gives answers through stories of people who are in need of a real and powerful Savior. This book is perfectly named because the stories are indeed relatable. If you are searching and in need of answers, in these pages you may see how, even with great intentions and huge desires, we may still manage to push God away. The One we love most, the One we cry out to, the One we say we trust, sometimes we don't recognize or accept when He's right there in our midst. This is us. *Relatable God* acts as a mirror, so that we can see ourselves in all of our brokenness. If we can finally see ourselves fully, we might just see, welcome, and embrace the One who has never left us and who has always seen us.

Angela Robinson,
Actress, Tyler Perry's
The Haves and the Have Nots

What People Are Saying About Relatable God

Donna Robinson understands the power of relating to a good story. And the stories in *Relatable God* draw us into real-life situations with God, providing a guidebook packed with wisdom and encouragement for life. Read this book and be reminded of God's love and presence with you in all of life's challenges.

Jennifer Camp,
Gather Ministries Co-Founder

☙

TABLE OF CONTENTS

※

Acknowledgements

ε⁄ɔ

First giving honor to God, Who is the Head of my life.
(SO churchy, I know. But honestly, I am nothing without Him!)

ε⁄ɔ

I also want to thank my loving parents,
who have always encouraged and influenced me. They worked
so hard to give my family the best life possible, and I am
forever grateful for their sacrifices. I thank God for my praying
grandmothers. My siblings, nieces, nephew, cousins and uncles,
thank you for believing in me. To my two Auntie Angela's - you
women are awesome, and such an inspiration.

ε⁄ɔ

I'd like to thank my Pastor,
Overseer Myra Jackson of Pilgrim Pentecostal Church of Christ.
You are a phenomenal woman who gave me such wisdom and
foresight about this book that it changed my way of thinking
about it. I appreciate you, 'Pastah'!

ε⁄ɔ

❦

To my accountability partner Lil' Rhan,
and to the women who have been my soul sisters: Courtenay,
Jeannie, Glendie, Candice, Kontesssa, Adebola, Keila, Cinthya,
Cortney and Perez...I love you all so much! Thank you for your
copious amounts of love and wisdom.

❦

Sis. Alice!
I would NOT have been able to finish this book without you.
I will never be able to thank you enough.

My dear friend Jessica Champeau:
your testimony of how God responded to your "what if I fail?"
with His "what if you fly" ...whew! That blessed me so good I
HAD to write about it. Thank you!

❦

To my book editors and publishers,
thank you for everything. Man, these saints sure know how
to publish and edit a book! I couldn't have asked for a better
company to work with.

❦

❦

I would also like to thank Pastor Jarris Shaw
of Kingdom Covenant Church. He once described a dream he
had in which he was resting on the moon as he talked with God.
His words created a picture in my mind that I will never forget.
I believe God desires us to see things from His perspective as He
sits high and looks low. This also prompted me to choose cover
art for this book that reflects being seated in heavenly places.

❦

Lastly, if you are reading this book
and have been inspired or touched in some way, I want to thank
you as well. Thank you for having an open heart and an open
mind. Continue reading, never stop learning, keep shining.
Remember, with God, NOTHING IS IMPOSSIBLE.

❦

※

Prologue

*H*ere we go! This may be the promotion I've been waiting for—I think.

Well, all I really know is I'm getting a new assignment. It's supposed to have a *big* impact. So it could be a promotion, a transfer, or ... anything. I don't know. My boss just mentioned it to me in passing the other day, and I've been anxious about our next meeting ever since. I've been praying for a promotion, though. Like, really, really praying for one.

I do my traditional hype-yourself-up-in-the-bathroom-mirror routine and then make my way to the meeting. I definitely don't want to be late.

Whew.

"Good morning, Boss. How are you today?" I ask.

"Good morning! Glad you asked. Today has honestly been quite troublesome. If only they would listen to me." He pauses for a moment then continues. "But thankfully, I have hard workers like you who step up to the plate and follow instructions. That always brightens up my world."

A deep smile spreads across my face. Bossman always has a way of seeing the bright side of things. As far as bosses are concerned, mine truly is the best. Over the years I've seen him go to the rescue at least a million times a day while getting blamed for things that were not his fault. And he doesn't always get the credit he deserves for the amazing things that he does. It's so unfair. He deserves nothing but the best. But like he said, I'm glad that my work helps balance things out a bit. My nervousness begins to disappear.

"*Sooo*, speaking of instructions...," I prod. Nothing like a good, solid transition to get straight to the point.

"Well for starters, you made yourself available and actually came to me and asked me what you could do for me. That's always the best way to start in my book. Once I saw that you were serious, I decided that it was time to let you know more about your assignment. I've actually been wanting you to do it for a while, but I didn't say anything until I knew you were ready. Now I can see that you're definitely ready. The instructions are pretty simple; I want you to write."

"Write? Like, *write* write?"

I'm beyond confused. I'd never been much of a writer, and I'm pretty sure he already knows that. A reader, yes (Team Bookworm!), but a writer? Nah, I don't think so. Simon Cowell's *It's a no from me* echoes in my head.

"I heard that, and yes I want you to write. I'm going to tell you what to write about as you go," he adds, pre-empting my next question about what I should be writing.

"Okay, so where do I even begin? When am I supposed to start?"

"Right now while it's still daytime. Because, you know, when night cometh—"

"No man can work," I respond, finishing his John 9:4 quote with a nod. "I know."

It's like I can feel him smiling, and I can't help but smile back. "So let me get this straight. I basically have to stop what I'm doing and just write?"

"Yes."

"Well, what about all the other things that you have me doing? I now have to add writing —about I don't even know what—to this list?"

I don't mean to badger him; I'm just trying to get an understanding. I have a ton on my plate already, so I'm a bit surprised that he's asking for more without giving specifics.

"You will multitask, of course. But this assignment is your main focus right now. It is very, very important," he explains patiently.

"Boss, how exactly am I going to do this though? Can you give me a little bit more detail? An outline maybe?"

"My dear, you just write. You write. That's it."

"But I don't know—"

"You do know how to write. In fact, you've been writing since you were four. I know because I just so happened to be there. It was cute."

He seriously has the best memory in the world.

"Okay. I'm feeling a little lost, but okay, I can do this." I say this more to myself now than to him.

I'm sensing that our meeting is coming to a close, but I'm no longer concerned about the time. Deep inside I'm beginning to feel that this could actually turn out to be the promotion I've been praying for. By no means does it look like a promotion right now, but somehow I believe that this is going to be big.

I already know what his response will be to my last question, but I ask anyway. "You'll help me out, right?"

"I always do, don't I? Because, you know, Luke 12:12 and all."

I smile.

For the Holy Spirit will teach you in that very hour what you ought to say.

Luke 12:12

Part I

HOW HE LOVES US

Down to Ride

*A*nother blood-curdling scream. My goodness. Really? The trip I'd been planning forever was not turning out the way I'd hoped it would.

"You're terrified," I said. "Your *one* job was to just sit back and ride. Your one job."

"I know, I know," she responded. "I am *so* down to ride. It's just that I'm more comfortable when I'm behind the wheel, that's all."

"But didn't you ask me to take this?" I tapped the steering wheel for emphasis. "You ask me to take it all the time. *Jesus take the wheel* is literally your favorite hashtag."

"Well, yeah, I did. But I was kinda hoping you'd still let me call the shots. You're not letting me do anything."

"That's the whole point of riding along, my dear. You don't have to do anything but ride along."

"But I want to drive now. It *is* my car, after all."

Her car? Oh, she tried it.

"Well technically it's not, but that's a whole 'nother conversation. The last time you forced your way back into the driver's seat, we got lost, ran out of gas, and barely got anything accomplished. Since I've been driving, we've been safe, making progress, you've had time to focus on things other than driving, and we made up for lost time. So tell me again why you're only comfortable when you drive?"

"Look, I'm not saying you're not doing a good job— you're doing a great job. But I just have a certain way I like doing things. When I'm not the one driving, I just can't seem to relax."

She shifted uncomfortably in the passenger seat and continued. "When you drive, I don't always know where we're going, and I have no control whatsoever. But when I drive, I at least have a bit of an idea of where we're going to end up."

"But regardless of where we go, how we get there, or where we end up, I'm with you. Doesn't that count for anything?" I asked. "When have I ever taken you somewhere and just left you hanging?"

She looked at me. Her expression showed me what was in her heart: she essentially was *not* down to ride as previously stated. Hmph.

"What more can I do to show you that I've got it under control? What will it take? Do you want me to give you my life or something?" I asked.

She chuckled. "Good one. But I just don't see why you won't let me drive and then you just tell me where to go. Why is it such a big deal? Either way, we're still moving."

"That's not how this works; that's not how any of this works," I replied, quoting the infamous Esurance commercial. "Listen; the point is to trust me. Trust is not the same thing as doing it your way with me falling in line behind you."

"I do trust you! Of course I trust you. I wouldn't even be here if I didn't trust you. I'd still be at home, stuck in the past.

But I'm here with you. What more do I have to do to prove I trust you?"

Don't you love when your kids try to use your same rhetoric on you? "You have to actually trust me, dear. That's how you prove you trust me."

"Ugh!" She folded her arms. "It's kinda messed up for you to say that I don't trust you after all this."

"Then prove it. Put your money where your mouth is."

She turned to the back seat and reached for the wallet in her purse.

"No, no dear, not literally. It's a figure of—look, what I'm saying is, show me that you trust me. I'm going to keep driving, and I want you to show me how much you trust me by how you sit back and ride. Sound like a deal?"

"Piece of cake," she said confidently.

***

She blew it. In less than two minutes, she blew it. Ah well. At least she tried. Sort of.

Right after we made our deal, I started to turn a corner, and the way she screamed you would've thought I had turned onto Elm Street. Scream Queen was *loud*. I mouthed *sorry* to the angels in heaven covering their ears.

The nails of her right hand dug into the side panel of the car. Her feet slammed on invisible brake pads, stretching her legs stiffly as she inched further down and back into her seat. Her teeth clenched hard as she braced for an impact that would never come. Had I not known any better, I would've looked around for the semi-truck that she clearly saw barreling toward us. But there was no semi-truck. No danger present whatsoever. I had simply turned a corner.

Definitely not the intimate bonding experience I had wanted. Imagine what it'd be like to spend a lifetime planning a surprise party for a loved one, they showed up, and then acted as if they were completely terrified the entire party. What if they had a look of terror in every selfie you took with them? That wouldn't be fun for the party planner or the guest of honor. Not fun at all.

I glanced over nonchalantly, as though her screams had not just reached the highest heaven. "You good?"

"Doing just fine," she hissed through clenched teeth. Her chest slowly heaved up and down, up and down. She repositioned herself in her seat over and over. Although she no longer braced herself for impact, she just had a hard time sitting still. The impulse to regain control over the ride fought her tooth and nail; the urge overwhelmed her entire body. Anyone who looked at her in that moment would immediately be able to tell she was stressed out.

The thoughts that raced through her mind were equally riotous:

Suggest using GPS, that way you'll know what's ahead.

Get carsick. Then He'll have to let you drive so that you don't throw up.

Just jump back in the driver's seat, sis.

"Piece of cake, right?" I asked, which purposely interrupted her thoughts.

"More like pieces of glass tearing through my chest." Her eyes were still wide-eyed as she continued to grip the side panel.

So dramatic.

"Okay, the way my trust game is set up, I don't want you to be this stressed about this ride," I explained. "I actually never wanted you to stress about it at all. The point of trusting me is to rest in me, relax in me. Trusting me should put your mind at ease because you trust that I've got your back. Trust that I've got everything under control. If trusting me doesn't give you peace, then that's a sign that you may not trust me completely."

I gave it a few moments to sink in before I continued. "Trust is something you can give me, like a gift. When you give someone a gift, it's for them to use and enjoy. You don't keep checking in and telling them what to do with their gift, how to use it, where to put it. No; you give it to them so they can do with it as they please. It's the same way when you trust me with something; it's for me to do what I want with it. You don't try and dictate what I do with it, call the shots, or any of that, because it's not yours anymore. It's mine. You gave it to me, so now it's mine and no longer yours."

"So basically I gave this whole journey over to you when I trusted you with it," she said. "Now this journey belongs to you, not me, and you're supposed to drive, not me."

"Exactly."

She remembered the night she prayed to me and asked me to help her surrender her life to me. She pictured herself that night as she prayed, cried, struggled to let go.

After she spent some time thinking of what happened that night, she began to open up. "I remember when I surrendered everything to you. I guess I'm not really living like I've surrendered. You must be tired of me checking in every two seconds, huh?"

"I actually understand why you do it, so don't feel bad. I get it. You feel as though I've let you down in the past, so you try to protect yourself from being disappointed again by staying in control. That's your mindset in a nutshell; control is basically your defense mechanism. But fortunately I'm nothing like the people you know; I'm not giving up on you no matter how long it takes. One day you're gonna see that trusting me is worth it."

I looked over to her with a smile. Being the awesome dad that I am, I continued to drive.

And she continued to scream.

And scream.

We continued to make progress, we continued to get closer to our destination, but she continued to scream. I mean, she *screamed*. Of course she repeated how much she trusted me, but she begged to drive again. We had several more one-on-ones about trust before I allowed her to take the keys.

"If you insist," I said.

Even with the upcoming detour, in my heart I knew that all this would eventually lead her to completely trust me.

I watched her settle comfortably back into the driver's seat. "One day, you'll truly be down to ride. Maybe not today, love, but one day."

"Like I said, I do trust you," she said with a smile. "I really do."

She sat happily behind the wheel that she asked me to take, and she made one wrong turn after another. We got nowhere.

Literally nowhere, cuz we ended up getting pulled over.

"Hello, ma'am; may I have your license and registration?" the officer asked.

She rolled her eyes as she gripped the steering wheel tightly. "Can I know why I'm being pulled over?"

"Failure to yield, ma'am."

As she closed her eyes, she silently replayed our conversation in her mind. It dawned on her that she had not fully yielded to me either.

She opened her eyes and peered over at me. "You win."

"I always do."

Scoliosis

You asked for help, but you're not gonna take *the help?* I thought about this as I watched my friend struggle, for the millionth time, to figure this thing out.

"I'm here if you need anything," I said, aware that he may never admit that he needed me.

"I know!" he shouted back.

At that point, I stopped walking altogether. My dear friend continued on his way without even noticing I had stopped. His gripes and complaints had drowned out the sound of my footsteps a while ago. He was so focused on doing it his way that his tunnel vision had pushed me out of the picture.

I watched him push and pull his monstrosity of a bag behind him. He constantly changed positions; he'd be in front pulling and then run behind to start pushing, a strenuous dance and waste of energy in the heat of the day. One time he pulled so hard that his shoulder popped. Legit *popped.* The sound scared him.

"Bones shouldn't pop like that," he said. "Or was that even my bone?"

Of course the minute I suggested he take a break and rest his snap, crackle, and popping shoulder, he claimed he had it under control. So he'd rather pop like a bag of popcorn than listen to the one he called for help. It made perfect sense.

"It's fine. It's *fine*," he said, apparently diagnosing himself as he'd done many times before. So now, not only did his shoulder hurt, his curved spine was a reminder that pain was real, and he needed to slow down. He'd pay attention to his body every now and then, stopping for a brief second to stretch and twist his torso as if that did anything to help. It definitely did not help. His stretches effectively aggravated his condition because one, he did them way too fast, and two, he didn't need to stretch at all. He just needed to *stop*.

For me it was like watching someone try tennis for the first time and completely ignore Serena Williams's free lesson. *Bruh, just* take *the help. It's okay!*

He continued to push. And pull. And occasionally, pop. But at least he encouraged himself. Well, not really. It was more like: *I'll just beat myself up until I finish, and then I'll probably congratulate myself when I'm done* kind of self-talk. But there's not really a word for that.

"Are you sure you don't want me to just—"

"*I said I'm fine!*" He turned his head to the right, expecting me to be there. When he realized I wasn't, he whirled around until his eyes locked with mine. "I got it!"

"But do you though?" The way he carried out this task showed me that he had asked for help he didn't really want to take. He said he needed help, but he didn't truly want it—at all.

It took him about ten minutes to take two steps. He had called me a while ago and beat around the bush about seeing if I were available, but he had held back what was really on his mind. He couldn't bring himself to admit that this was too much for him to do on his own and he needed a friend to come through. But of course I made myself available as I'd always done.

We could've finished a long time ago. He could've finished his day pain-free and stress-free. Honestly, he didn't have to do this at all. My dear friend, beautiful but stubborn. Focused but on the wrong things. Our interactions usually went something like this:

Me: Okay, so instead of staying upset about that, why don't you just talk to her and see her point of view? Then, you can let her know how you feel and that will—

Him: What?! Who cares what she thinks? I ain't tellin' her nothin'!

or

Him: I'm never gonna let him live this down.

Me: But what if the shoe was on the other foot? How would you feel if someone constantly reminded you of your past mistakes?

Him: Well, I'm human. I can forgive, but I won't forget!

or

Me: Okay, so here's exactly what you need to do: just put this here first, then drop it off there, and it's done.

Him: No. Instead I'm gonna open it up, completely rewire it, figure out how to put it back together myself, take it twenty other places, and then tie it to a bald eagle and hope it finds it's way back to me. Yeah, that's what I'll do. Thanks!

So yeah, I'll wait. Maybe one day he'll get it. At least he called me this time. He usually doesn't even do that. Maybe next time he calls me for help, he'll actually *take* my help.

Kthxbye

*F*inally.

After binge-watching yet another Netflix series (Really, my guy? Since when do you like tigers mixed with drama?), you wake up with excitement. Interesting. That's not how you usually wake up.

I'd like to think you're excited because we get a chance to talk after all this time. You've been pretty busy, and I've been waiting. So yes, I guess you could say your excitement has rubbed off on me. We have so much to talk about. But first, I want to let you know that—

Oh, hi Facebook. That again. So you were excited to check the comments from your post about the tiger guy. That's what put the spring in your step this morning. Go figure.

Okay, enough with your scrollin', buddy; let's get to it. I want to tell you about how—

Are you *really* laying back down right now? Just like that, huh? No, don't get comfortable; that's the devil talking. Hey, stop fluffing your pillow!

Wow. So you only woke up to check Facebook, possibly start a fight in the comments, and slide into two DMs. You woke up for *that*? We didn't even get to finish our dream sequence. You woke up before the best part.

And now you're just gonna go back to sleep like we didn't have a meeting set? Hmph. You're already snoring. But you'll be up again in a few minutes. Man, are you blessed to get these new mercies every day. Cuz if not, you'd be in some serious trouble. Let's try this again.

Well, of course now you're running late for work. Don't you get tired of waking up in panic mode and having to skip breakfast? But yet you continue to mismanage your time and I'm the one that gets left out of your day.

I don't like being pushed to the side, you know. How would you like it if your barber rescheduled at the last minute every single time and didn't tell you until after you'd already showed up at his shop?

So now you're hungry, swamped with work, and low-key looking for another job unbeknownst to anyone in your circle. So there's that.

Oh, you didn't say grace at lunch because your co-workers were around? Not even a rushed lunchtime prayer today. Wow.

Uh-oh. Did I speak too soon? (That was rhetorical; I never do.) We've got some action here. Looks like you're going away to get some time by yourself. You finally remembered to talk to me.

About the new job you want.

You want a new job, and you trust me to come through for you.

Oh. Okay.

The thing is I trust every short, hurried word you just said. I know you trust me to do it for you. At least you know that you need me. You always come to me when you need something because you know I can handle it. So I know you believe in me. I don't doubt that at all.

But why is this the only time we talk? I remind you every day that we need to talk, but you give me a bunch of reasons why you don't have time for me, yet you make time for everyone and everything else. It's been so long since we really had a heart-to-heart, and it's not like I haven't been waiting for you. So that I can explain things to you. And comfort you. And prepare you for what's ahead. Because little do you know, most of this won't even be here in a few months. The whole world is about to get shut down, and I've been trying to prepare you for it. Yet you are asking me about a new job when truthfully, the online business idea I gave you last year is what you need to focus on. But conversations involve two parties, not just one.

It hurts you that your family only speaks to you when they need money or some other favor, yet this is the same way you've been treating me. And what makes it even worse is that I already know I won't hear from you again until you get laid off two weeks from now. I know because I just know.

So long story short, I heard your prayer. You're just too busy to hear my answer.

Big Mad

"**A**nd another thing," he announced his re-entry into the one-way conversation he was having because he clearly did not want me to speak. "I do things without you *all* the time, almost every day. And the only time I even think of bringing you into the picture is when I need to blame you for something that doesn't go my way. Can you please explain to me what's wrong with that? I find it completely normal, but apparently you don't, which makes no sense to me at all. If I purposely make a decision that leads to disaster, why in the *world* should I have to deal with the consequences?"

He walked back and forth in slow strides with the air of an experienced trial lawyer and continued to plead his case. "Prime example. The other day, I'm having lunch with my friend. She asks me if she should try out the steakhouse that just opened up, and I tell her no, she shouldn't go to the steakhouse because she's vegan, and they aren't going to have many vegan options there. What does she do?"

He spun around for dramatic effect, waving his arms wildly. He's *so* extra.

"She goes to the new steakhouse. And of course she calls me and complains about how much of a waste of time that was. And of course she has to spend extra money to Uber to another restaurant where she can actually get some decent rabbit food to eat." He chuckled dryly. "And she blames me for the horrible night she ended up having. Of course she does! Now, was she wrong asking for my advice, doing the exact opposite of what I suggested, then having the audacity to blame me for the outcome? *Absolutely!* Just cancel the whole friendship at this point. But when it comes to me and you, these rules don't apply. My friend is wrong for not taking my advice and then blaming me for the disaster, but when I don't take your advice and then blame you for the disaster, it's perfectly fine. *Comprendé*, amigo?"

His Spanish accent was so bad that it didn't even sound Spanish. However, I did appreciate that he was saying what most people refuse to admit: basically, I can get blamed for everything under the sun, even when I tell people ahead of time what will work and what won't, but they shouldn't be held responsible for anything—ever.

"And I totally get that I wouldn't be here if you hadn't helped me and forgiven me and all that jazz, but how dare you ask me to help someone else when I have my own life to live? How inconsiderate is that? And on top of that, you want me out here *forgiving* people? All someone has to do is blow me off one time and we are *done*. Finished. Finito."

Not sure he realized that word wasn't even Spanish. (Did he get the memo that Duolingo was free?) In any event his argument was tragic, just tragic. Almost as tragic as his foreign language skills.

"So again, I get that you want things a certain way, and I'm supposed to do this, that, and the third, but enough is enough. Me being a self-proclaimed good person according to my own standards should suffice. Case closed."

And with that he marched back out of the door for the third time, being welcomed again with a round of applause from millions of like-minded individuals who support this logic too.

So here is what I gathered from this "logic":

Key Takeaways

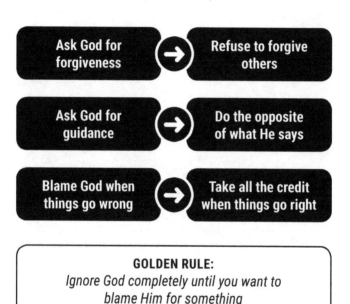

GOLDEN RULE:
Ignore God completely until you want to blame Him for something

Oh. My. Self.

And I'm supposed to be okay with this logic? Really?

Behind the Scenes

"I'm still going to prove you wrong," the devil said in defiance. "Even if I can't kill him, I'll still show you that you're wrong."

I rolled my eyes. After all this time, he still acted like he knew more about my kids than I do. I dismissed the evil one from my presence.

"Boy, bye." With a short wave of my hand, I sent him six cubits backwards into the air.

I turned my attention back to my child and studied him carefully. I could sense the fast heartbeat in his chest, the cloudiness in his mind from many sleepless nights, his nervous, timid spirit.

Whispering softly to his soul, I said, "I *am* here. Focus on me."

***

In an instant Trey finally opened his mouth.

"It seems like the second I get the courage to stand back up, something comes and knocks me down again. I just don't see the point of all this anymore. I feel like it's just getting worse. In a matter of days, I've seen the ugliest side of people—of humanity even—and it's devastating. How could someone who loves me just walk completely out of my life? I don't think I'll ever get over that one. It's like I could feel my heart being pulled apart, very slowly. That hurt me so bad. And I'm just tired of hurting. I want it to stop. I feel like I have nothing left. Every day I live feeling like life could just happen, and the next small thing is just gonna send me over the edge. I can't take anymore. And now I don't even have someone to love. I just wanted one thing to keep me happy, but I can't have even that.

"God, I just needed *one* thing to help me through this. I'm not trying to say You're not enough, because You definitely are. It's just that I wanted someone here to love me through this. To cry to. To help me. The whole world is happily married to someone they met at the bar while they were both drunk, and I'm here alone, struggling with everything by myself. Everything falls on my shoulders; there's no one here to help carry my load. Why couldn't I just have *one* thing?

"I'm always by myself, and I can't stand it. This isn't what I wanted. I mean, I knew it wouldn't be easy, but *this*? I just need a break. I keep hearing about this breakthrough, but honestly, where is it? I know I haven't been perfect, but have I really been so bad that I deserve all this? So if I'm being punished, then that's one thing, but truthfully, this feels like torture. I get hurt by things that probably wouldn't phase anybody else, and I hate it. It's like I'm cursed for having a big heart.

"Sometimes I just wish I didn't love anymore. What am I supposed to do?"

***

Trey's prayer squeezed my heart. In the distance I saw the devil and his demons preparing for another attack. (They really worked as though I couldn't see and hear everything they did.) They planned to keep Trey tossing and turning all night, and they also wanted to flood his mind with worst-case scenarios that would interrupt my conversation with him.

I closed my eyes and continued whispering to Trey's heart.

***

"So, this is me, praying for a miracle. Funny that the simple things would be a miracle right now: sleep, an appetite, at least *one* good day. That's what state my life is in right now. I'm so desperate that it would be a miracle to just have one good day.

I'm not the best at this praying thing, but I really hope you hear me, God. I feel like I can't take anymore. My family, my friends, my life—it's just too much!"

***

The main line buzzed. I turned around and gave my literal wingman the universal head nod.

"Roger that," he said and turned to the team. "We just got the green light. Everyone, all systems go!"

An alarm sounded that pushed everyone into motion. Almost immediately the worship leaders put down their lattés, took off their non-prescription glasses, and began to sing. The musicians joined in shortly after. In one section the seamstresses began working on the fabric that would be added to my robe, and the content team drafted the inscription that would be written on it. A small but mighty event planning team started organizing the afterparty, while one of them flew over to the scoreboard and added another number to our side.

In a different area a group ran to collect weaponry, and one member from that group brought me a sword, which

I promptly sharpened. The archangels did their infamous group huddle to coordinate a plan of attack. I heard their team instructions over the bustle of all the other activity.

"All the enemy can do is resist; they can't win. So our main goal is to destroy their resistance. That's it."

From below I heard Trey's familiar voice crying. "Are you going to do anything about this?"

I smiled. "Oh, you bet I am."

Then he said to me, "Do not fear, Daniel, for from the first day that you set your heart to understand, and to humble yourself before your God, your words were heard; and I have come because of your words."

Daniel 10:12

On to the Next

"Almost there. Almost," I thrust my shoulder into the tall, heavy door, "*there.*"

"Wait!" came a scream from below.

"Wait?"

Frantic, she looked up at me, her eyes wide with panic. "Just one last peek, please? Just one more, okay?" She pleaded with me without technically asking.

We could have finished a while ago, but she'd been dead-set on getting her "last" peek—several times, in fact—her final goodbyes, her closure. Out of all the instructions, parables, and proverbs, not once have I said anything about needing closure in order to move on. Yet she and so many others swear that closure is what they need. Goodness!

Ah well. I knew that she would close the door when she was ready to close it. It was her door, after all. I was there to help whenever she was ready, even though I wished she was ready now.

This time her last peek ended up lasting five months—five long, hard, unnecessary months. It was painful to watch, but she had insisted on going back and I'm not one to stand in her way. The good thing is, she ended up running back out this time. Literally running. She had never come out like that before. She was usually sad and remorseful, almost afraid to take each step that led her farther from what she was leaving behind. But not this time. When she ran out, she practically begged me to shut the door as fast as I could.

"Okay, okay," I said. "Let's give it one final push on the count of three."

"I'm ready!" she said eagerly, almost angrily.

"One, two, three—push!"

We threw ourselves against the door. It ground slowly before closing for good. The dust and debris that rose into the air as it clamped shut made her cough and heave. Fortunately I had some trusty well water on hand, and I gave her some. She drank it thirstily and then leaned back against the closed door.

"Don't get too comfortable, my love." I pulled her toward me. "I've got something I want to show you right now."

She was resistant. "I'm tired. Can we wait until later? I just got here."

"I know you did, but we're already behind schedule. This time it took you five whole months before you came back out."

"I'm sorry. I really am."

As her father I knew there was some truth to her apology. She was sorry for going against what I told her to do, and she was also sorry for how things turned out when she went back. But I wanted her to realize that her desire to go back is what we really needed to talk about. Even though she didn't want to go back anymore, that didn't change the fact that she *wanted* to go back. I was capable of taking away that desire, but she would first have to surrender it to me. Without fully grasping that this needed to be addressed, she ran the risk of disobeying me again.

I preferred a complete uncovering—from her lips—of everything that had happened from start to finish so that we could work through each piece together. That is what leads to transformation. But transformation is a process, one that I am committed to. I had been trying to show her the benefits of listening to me, but she lived as though she had everything figured out.

"I just had to …," she trailed off, knowing that it would be impossible to lie to me.

I gently coaxed her. "I'm listening."

"I just needed closure. I felt like if I just up and left, then I would always wonder what could have been, what would have happened. I needed to get that off my chest before I left for good. I really did. I know it would have bothered me for years if I didn't do it. I hope you understand. I'm so sorry."

Thankfully, at least now I had her confession. In her own words, and by spending a little more time with me, we reached a true confession of the heart behind her actions. That was a great place to start.

"My dear, I just asked you to close the door, not go back and *get* closure."

"I know. It's just hard. I really tried, but it's hard."

"But it's not hard when I'm the one handling it." I explained this as though I was explaining it for the very first time. Because I wanted her to get it. I wanted it to finally sink in this time.

"I appreciate you so much. You are always so patient with me." She reached up to grab my hand. "Just stay with me one more night. I promise we can go first thing in the morning. I'm just so tired. That last trip took so much out of me." She leaned back against the door, pulled me close, and laid her head on my shoulder.

Even though I wanted to show her what I had for her, I understood why she was tired. Her last trip back had truly taken a toll on her.

I was content to just be with her, even if she insisted on staying outside a closed door.

***

So she wasn't ready for another journey just yet. But honestly, I had never told her we were going on a journey: I simply told her that I wanted to show her something. She assumed that she had to take another journey because her previous decision to go back turned into a journey by itself, one that I never meant for her to take. So now because her last journey was so hard, she had mentally developed an excuse to stay right where she was.

And this, my friends, was a prime example of a misunderstanding: I said one thing, she assumed I meant something else without asking me for clarification, and she moved ahead of me based on her assumption and not my instruction. Oh, the importance of good communication!

So she rested, and we talked just like she wanted. The good thing was she didn't reopen that door, even though we continued to sit right outside of it. The downside was, we weren't making any progress at all. We were just…there.

We ended up staying outside the door for a month. And even when I reminded her about the time that had passed, she replied with the usual one-liners:

I'm tired.

I'm not ready.

What's so bad about where I am right now?

Can't we just do it tomorrow?

My sweet, dear child. Bless her heart. Just bless her little heart.

"Okay, love, how about this? We can stay here with our backs pressed up against a door that we closed one month ago for as long as you want. If you want to stay here, I'll stay with you. If you want to see what I have for you, I'll show you. I'll be with you no matter what you decide. Now, I'm happy that you don't want to go back anymore, but the longer you sit outside this closed door, the more you might be tempted to go back. Remember, it all started with you just wanting to take a peek inside, and from there you wanted to just check in and see how things were going. Before you knew it, you were in over your head. You never intended to get caught back up in there again, but you did. So staying here is eventually going to lead you back down that same road. That's why it's best to receive what I have for you next. I have something I really want to show you, but I won't force it. That's not my style. So it's up to you, my love. Let me know what you want to do."

Now the proverbial ball had been placed in her court. For emphasis, and because props are always in order, I placed a round ball neatly in her hands. It was my hope that she would slam dunk it into the hoop that was just within her reach.

***

Three months later and she was still there, rolling that same ball back and forth. Yikes. *Anything* can become a distraction when motivation is lacking.

And then out of somewhere, it happened: "Daddy, I want something different. I'm ready for something new."

Finally! It was music to my ears!

"Well, what do you have in mind?"

"I feel like I need to be doing something else, I just don't know what. I'm just tired of being here, I guess."

"Well, do you want me to show you something?" As a parent, sometimes if you package your request a bit differently, your child will agree with you without even realizing it. It will *hit different*, as the kids these days say.

"Yes, you know I love surprises!"

I hadn't seen her this excited in years. "Okay then, let's go."

And just like that we were off. If only she got this excited every time I had something to show her. It seemed like she was the most responsive when everything made logical sense to her. I had been teaching her to just trust me without demanding all the answers upfront, but we still had a way to go with that lesson. Maybe this experience would show her why it's best to just let go and trust me.

What I had to show her was a relatively short distance from the closed door. In fact it was only a few steps away, so we made it there in no time. She was a bit confused when we stopped since we hadn't gone that far, but I was so elated she was finally moving that I didn't mind at all. She was about to see why the last closed door was so necessary.

***

"Another door?" She sounded as though she was on the verge of tears.

"Yes, that's what it looks like. What's wrong?"

"You said you had something to show me. I was expecting a surprise, something big, not another door."

"My friend, you should have more faith and more hope. You should just have—more. Before you fall out in despair, please note that this door is only closed because we haven't opened it yet. It's simply a door that I want you to open; that's it. But this time I want you to open it *with* me."

Her expression was unchanged, and her arms remained folded.

"So, there are a few options on the table: we can open this door together, we can stay outside of it, or you can try to open it by yourself if you don't want my help. There's only one condition, though. You absolutely cannot go back to where you were. Going back is completely off limits."

No props this time. Just a short and simple list of options. I could see that she was thinking about what I said. She always does this cute thing where she scrunches her face together when she's in deep thought. She did it again, and I low-key loved it. I turned around to hide my smile.

"I guess I've been kind of a brat, haven't I?"

"Your words, not mine."

"I didn't mean to be this way. I've just been through a lot. That last place I was in was really rough. Even after all that, it was still hard for me to leave," she confessed.

"I know. I was there too, remember?"

"Yes, we talked every night. When we talked it was the only time everything didn't just…hurt."

"It was hard for me to see you hurt like that." I walked over to her and placed my hand on her shoulders. My touch made her soul exhale. "I want you to get what I have for you. You say you're not ready, but I know you are. So it's really all up to you. Even if you don't want my help, I'm not going anywhere anytime soon. I love you."

She thought for a moment. Then she placed her hands in mine and looked up at me, beaming. "Let's do this. I'm ready."

I looked down at her for a while, taking in the moment. Her expression was priceless. She had no idea what was up ahead, but from the looks of it, she wasn't concerned about that at all. She just wanted what I had for her, and she wanted me there with her. She had finally gotten to the point where she was ready for anything, and I absolutely loved it.

I took her hand. "Okay, then. Let's go."

We ran toward the door. On the count of three, we gave it a big pull. Almost immediately light began to shine from beneath the heavy door, which had barely moved from our effort. It would take a lot more pulling to get it completely open, but that was quite alright. Each time she pulled showed me how much she wanted what I had for her, how much she trusted me without even knowing all the details.

She looked at the gold light flowing from the bottom of the door then stared up at me in an excited state of confusion. She could already tell that what I had waiting for her was more than she could ever ask for or even think. Together we had opened the door to the very first day of her new life.

"Daddy ..."

"I told you to just follow me. Let's go!"

Bombs Away

*D*aniel's morning alarm rang in his ears, causing every cell in his body to roll their eyes in annoyed molecular unison. He swatted his bedsheets away, only to continue lying in place, his mind racing. *It's kinda hard to sleep when people keep bothering you,* he thought. He eventually made his way to his bathroom mirror in an attempt to put himself together. Almost immediately he noticed the familiar tightness around the upper part of his chest. For some reason today it seemed a bit tighter than usual. The tightness caused his shoulders to slouch just a bit, so he had to make an extra effort to stand up straight. Throughout the day he would constantly readjust himself, only to realize moments later that he was slouching again.

Getting old sucks.

It was more palatable for him to blame it on age than consider the possibility of a heart condition or the coronavirus.

Now time to make the glorious morning commute to my wonderfully pleasant job.

He loved to humor himself—fake it 'til you make it, right? Almost as soon as he stepped onto the sidewalk, three kids circled him and began flicking cigarette lighters on and off.

They sang an eerie melody at the top of their lungs, which sharply contrasted with the softness of their young voices.

"Get away from me, you little demons!" *Ugh. Kids these days — just completely out of order. And what genius parents let their kids play with lighters?* He shook his head in disgust.

Daniel readjusted himself and continued on his way. He could still hear the kids and their stupid little demon song, but fortunately the hustle and bustle of city life helped drown them out. As he walked, he made a point to look at the faces of the people who passed him by. Every day he amused himself by making up stories based on the facial expressions of those he passed by. He really got a kick out of doing that, and it helped make the commute a bit more bearable. Sometimes he would get so caught up in his made-up stories that he would laugh out loud, but everyone was usually too busy to notice when he did. Today he saw some typical city characters: the over-caffeinated millennial on her way to yoga class; old-money Medina that's too rich to say *excuse me* when he bumps into people; and of course the I'm So Important and Busy intern with his mask on upside down.

As Daniel was about to amuse himself with the next passerby, for the first time he struggled to conjure up something. He was thrown off by her intense stare at his chest. He watched her watch him and instinctively looked down to see what she could possibly be looking at. He saw nothing. He looked up again, and she was gone.

What a weirdo, with her didn't-get-the-memo-that-it's-rude-to-stare looking self.

He refocused on his next victim, who happened to be Will Ferrell's Spanish twin. Then only moments later it happened again. Another staring jerk.

And this one has the audacity to stop dead in his tracks!

The guy was an older gentleman who looked like he could be the world's best granddad, but the way he just stopped and stared took away the whole grandfatherly vibe he had going for him. The man almost seemed shocked. He eventually snapped out of his staring fit and hurried on his way.

All thoughts of Daniel's name game disappeared as he wondered what that little episode was all about. And then the demon kids returned, still singing their creepy song and flicking their lighters. He immediately turned around and skillfully positioned his leg in such a way that one of the kids tripped and fell over it.

"Oh no, be careful," he said in mock concern.

Little did they know he was an expert in tripping people's kids. Worked every time.

When he turned back around to continue his walk, he came face-to-face with a teenage girl standing right in front of him.

"Please, before it's too late!" she warned, reaching for his hand.

He snatched his hand away. "What does that even mean?"

The South Side of Chicago in him began to rise up, and he could feel frustration pulsing through his veins. The girl didn't respond; she just continued to stare dead into his eyes.

"Move!" He purposely brushed his shoulder against hers as he stormed off.

In the era of social distancing, it was wildly inappropriate to touch someone you didn't know, and the girl hadn't been wearing a mask, either.

I don't have time for this. What is everyone smoking today? First the stare contests, and now this?

He stopped at his favorite coffee shop and headed straight to the bathroom. Over the past few months, Daniel had worked to control his anger and wanted to calm himself down before he exploded at the next person who spoke to him. He never took time outs like this before he started working on his temper, so the fact that he was doing so was a pretty big deal. A huge deal in fact, given his past explosive temperament.

He splashed cool water on his face in an attempt to quench the fire in his veins, and then he looked at himself in the mirror. "I've barely even started my day, and I'm already on the verge of wanting to kill someone," he said to his reflection.

And this, my friends, is when the infamous spotlight shines on the main character and everything else fades to black. Daniel is here, looking at himself in a coffee shop mirror, wondering what was going on and more importantly, wondering *who* to ask what's going on.

Well, Daniel, this is what happens when you walk around with a bomb strapped to your chest. A legit *bomb*. Yes, that tightness in your chest is from the bomb you've been carrying this whole time.

Taking in a huge gulp of air, Daniel slowly backs one step away from the mirror. And then another. And another. And that's when he sees it. With his upper torso now in full view in the mirror, he can see a neatly placed bomb strapped around his chest. His eyes grow wide as a muffled scream escapes his throat. He doesn't dare look down for fear that he may see on his body what he sees in the mirror.

Paralyzed with fear, he is too afraid to move, but he knows he has to do something immediately. There's a bomb on his chest! His eyes frantically dart around the bathroom, his chest becoming tighter and tighter with each breath.

"Someone, please help me!"

His legs feel glued to the floor. He's breathing so hard he can't tell whether or not there's a familiar ticking sound coming from the bomb, but even if there is no sound, he wants this thing off him *now*. It's not until after he screams for help that he realizes that whoever comes to his rescue will likely mistake him for a terrorist.

Despite that concern he screams again in desperation. "Someone, *help*!"

Friend, do you really want just anyone to come to your rescue? *Someone* could be a person with no emergency training whatsoever, or it could even be those kids with the lighters. Who do you really need to call to *diffuse* this situation? In times like these, you better be sure someone who actually knows what to do comes to your rescue.

Daniel finally takes his eyes away from the mirror and looks down at his chest. He sees that each piece of dynamite contains a letter. When read from right to left, the letters spell *unforgiveness*.

"Who did this to me? Who did this?!"

Notice how one of the first things you do is find someone to blame for your situation? Let's take a step back and take all the guesswork out of this scenario because, let's be honest, no one likes to try and guess their way through something. You had yet another restless night because *people keep bothering you*. You woke up and immediately felt a tightness in your chest that you've felt for some time, but not once have you inquired about why that pain was there. Then as soon as you step outside, you are surrounded by imps that literally try to set you off. But instead of focusing on yourself, you focus on making them stop what they're doing with their lighters.

Think about that for a moment. You're the one with the deadly device, yet you wanted others to put their tiny, insignificant lighters away. That's basically like pointing out someone's splinter when you have an entire log in your own eye.

Now, fortunately there were some people who saw what you were carrying, one of whom even warned you that soon it would be too late. But instead of examining yourself to see what they saw, you became frustrated and angry with them because you did not understand. Again, you focused on what you thought was wrong with them instead of focusing on the issue you had.

Daniel begins having flashbacks of the people he had seen that morning. *How could I be so blind?*

My friend, this is the unfortunate result of unforgiveness; it squeezes you so much that it blinds you. People and situations come that are designed to light your fuse. Constant triggers and frustrations are aimed straight for your peace day-after-day. So much so that you get angry with those who were sent to help you because you can't even see that you *need* help. But even when you don't see it yourself, you feel it, so you know it's there. That, Daniel, is the heart of unforgiveness.

"What? I forgive people all the time. I'm a forgiving person!"

Yes, you are very capable of doing it, and you have done it, but in words only. You spoke forgiveness with your mouth, but you never took the action of taking the bomb off your chest. You still carry unforgiveness with you. It's been weighing you down.

"So I don't get any credit for trying? How is that fair?"

Your trying has *definitely* been rewarded. You're still alive, right?

"Well, yeah, I'm alive. But probably not for long because there's a freakin' bomb strapped to my chest!"

That is exactly the point. You have in fact been living with a bomb strapped to your chest, a very dangerous combination indeed. However, only you can make the decision to take it off. And once you take it off, you must also make the decision to not put it back on again. Keeping it off will require a continual commitment on your part. It's up to you to make sure the bomb stays off. The choice is yours to make. But I'm here to help, by the way. I *am* the expert.

His body slumps, and he sinks to his knees. "Well, can you help me take it off? I'll do whatever it takes."

Of course, that's what I'm here for. I needed you to see how important this is, how refusing to forgive literally causes your life to hang in the balance. We both know what happens to bombs that detonate: they destroy everything, including you.

"I promise I get it. I get it now. Whatever I have to do, I'll do it. I won't put it back on, I promise. Just please, help me."

You've been helped, my friend. You've been allowed to see and feel what's really happening inside of you. The real test comes when you have the opportunity to act on what you now know. Will you respond differently, or will you be the same way you were before?

"Of course I'll be different! How is that even a question? There's no way I want to go through this again."

My sentiments exactly. Very well. Make the best of this opportunity you've been given. You have the chance, and the choice, to live differently. It's my hope that you remember this place and never, ever return to it. And the best part is this: you won't have to go through this alone. I *am* the best at helping people out of bad situations.

Daniel begins feeling the tightness in his chest slowly disappear, and he inhales deeply. "I don't know what to say. Thank you. I know I don't deserve another chance, but thank you for giving me one anyway."

***

Leaving the coffee shop still a bit perplexed, Daniel begins to relish the thought of getting a new start.

Wow. I was really out here about to risk it all.

"And for what?" he says aloud. "Just to end up hurting myself with all this? No, definitely not. Never going back there again."

A young woman looks at Daniel strangely as she walks by, confused as to why he was talking to himself.

Now that's embarrassing. A bit of my own medicine, I suppose. Welp, at least she's not staring at a bomb strapped to my chest.

***

Agreed.

Now, when Daniel wakes up from this dream, he'll have a better understanding of the root cause behind many of his struggles. Fortunately he'll have another chance to forgive and let go while he still has time, because I've graced him with another chance. Now he knows how close to destruction he really was.

Last night could have easily been his last night.

Notice _Me_

"**D**uh, I can't wear a part cuz my forehead is too big."

Frustrated, she ran the comb back through her hair, praying that she'd still have edges after all the pulling she'd been doing. She spent several minutes trying to reorganize her thick, curly hair into a nice, twisted up-do. Her arms were beyond tired, the blood having drained from her arms long ago as she struggled to style her hair.

It's not that she didn't love her natural hair—she really did. It was just refusing to cooperate this time. Placing her hands on the sink to give her arms a rest, she eyed the row of wigs in the closet behind her.

Throwing one of my friends on would be clutch right now.

Echoes of hair salon chatter skipped back and forth through her mind as she took one step toward her closet.

Yassss, c'mon hair.

You cute, sis!

I see you; long hair don't care.

"Aht aht." Her eyes snapped back to her reflection in the mirror. "Short hair, _still_ cares." She resumed styling her hair. "If he doesn't like my natural look, then I'm probably not gonna like him, either."

She continued the methodical work on her tresses until they were finally placed into a high ponytail, her curls flowing tightly from the crown of her head. Of course she settled on the style that could've taken just five minutes had she not gone through fifty 'leven options beforehand.

"Pull it together, sis. You already doin' too much," she cautioned herself, reaching for her makeup bag. As her eyes scanned each shade of lipstick, she considered the potential message that each one might send to her date. She calculated the risks and benefits of each one as if it were an important life decision.

Nude doesn't stand out enough. And I'm tryna stand out.

Dark brown means I'm way too deep. I mean, I am, but still…

Bright red just looks like sex. Let me just throw this one away, then.

Clear lip gloss it is.

"Good thing I picked out my outfit last week," she said to herself as she applied the rest of her makeup. "See, I'm proactive. I plan ahead. Total wifey material."

Stepping back from the mirror, she examined herself from head to toe. Ever so slowly, her eyes went up, down, then back up again. The finished product looked amazing, but her nerves were now shot. Getting dressed was supposed to be fun, not hectic and stressful. In the amount of time it had taken her to get ready, she had called herself fat, given up at least five times, agonized over whether her dress was too frilly, and literally pulled out pieces of her hair in an attempt to get it done. *It took all that just to get ready for a first date?* She had forced herself to look absolutely perfect at the expense of tearing herself down.

The realization settled in as she began cleaning up the mess she'd made in her bedroom and bathroom. "Wow...I did all this just so he'll notice me."

That was it. She just wanted to be noticed. Behind her battle with herself was the fiery desire to not just be seen, but to be *noticed* (because there *is* a difference). After so much heartbreak, rejection, and disappointment, being *noticed* by the one she desired would really make all the difference.

For some time she had wanted a real love, an old-school romance. She had recently gotten to the point in her prayers where she was comfortable saying that she wanted a relationship, but she was still struggling to admit that she was afraid of being in love again. Both friendships and relationships had birthed a fear of real love, bringing her to a place where she was praying for something that she wasn't sure she was ready to receive.

Something strange had been happening lately; she was starting to listen to love songs again. For her that was a big step. Certain music always turned her mind to what could have been, and she would end up staying in that headspace for far too long—we all know that memories can just *ruin* certain songs. But now she was able to listen to love songs and just vibe without overthinking. The love songs helped her to see there was a certain experience she wanted to have again. She wanted to take part in the timeless phenomenon of *talking* to someone, the period right before you officially start dating. She wanted to gush to her girlfriends about her special someone, to have a reason to finally change her relationship status on Facebook. In essence, she wanted to be booed up.

But one thing she really wanted was the feeling of finding out that the one she had her eyes on was also interested in her.

Back in the day there was nothing like finding out that your secret crush had been asking around about you too. And oh, when you got that first note from them in class, the excitement of being asked to circle *yes* or *no* was one of the best parts. You always remember that first feeling, even if what happens after you circle *yes* doesn't go as planned.

The expectation, having someone to look forward to—she wanted all that again. And this evening was the first step toward what she really wanted, what she had been praying for. She hadn't felt this way about anyone in a long time. Before, one of the most time-consuming things about the men that pursued her was figuring out how to let them down easily. But this one was an exception. She liked him so much that it legit made her nervous. So nervous that when they first met, she geeked out and talked about foreign policy the whole time. Now *that's* nervous.

But thank God for another chance. She felt blessed to spend time with him again. She vowed not to make it sound like a business transaction this time. She also vowed to just do her best because she already cared about him.

"I really like him, and it's okay," she repeatedly told her timid heart.

Thoughts of how devastated she would feel if he didn't notice her popped up now and again, but those thoughts didn't consume her. Sure, it would suck if he weren't into her, if he brushed her to the side. The thought of having to start all over again if this didn't work out was hard; getting the courage to put herself out there again would probably take some time.

But what if this went right? What if he was just as interested in her as she was in him? She remembered her friend Jessica sharing a story about how she had prayed and asked God: *But what if I fail?*, and God's response was: *What if you fly?* That part was what she allowed her heart to hope for.

She still had no idea what he thought about her, but she definitely wanted him to notice her. Like, not just see her, but *notice* her.

***

I get it. I totally get it. I know exactly how she feels.

Watching her reminds me of a young entrepreneur I know. His name is Jayce. He's the IT equivalent of a starving artist. And boy did he love his craft. He was the type to take small jobs just so he could fund his passion. He had developed a financial intelligence app that could trace dirty money and alert police agencies all over the world. There were a million ways to combat money laundering, but he had discovered the easiest and most efficient way to do it. His app was designed to put an end to this in countries all over the world.

Jayce just needed at least one person to believe in him and his vision. He had all the blueprints, contracts, marketing strategies—everything but the money to get it up and running. He had spent all his time getting everything else in order so that by the time he finally got the money he needed, there would be no delay in launching his app.

Jayce reminded himself daily: *This could save lives. This app could help put violent kleptocrats and war criminals in jail. The world needs this app.* In the lonely absence of a solid support system, he had learned to encourage himself with this affirmation. His genuine desire was to help promote world peace, not to get rich. It truly bothered him that criminals could launder money, kill innocent people, and get away with it. He felt like he had to do something to stop this. It seemed so unfair that people like him who genuinely wanted to do the right thing couldn't even afford to be altruistic, while people who only cared about making more money were the ones doing just that. Almost daily he had to choose between paying his bills or using what little money he had to market his app, and the choice was always a hard one.

His daily affirmations were often overrun by doubts that constantly buffeted his mind. *I can't even afford to help change the world* was one of his most reoccurring thoughts. Yet each day he tried, each day he worked, each day he prayed for a miracle.

As he left the store where he stocked shelves at night, Jayce's mind wandered back to his app. *It doesn't even have to be a big break. I actually don't want anything major. I just need one investor who believes in this, who sees the value in my work. Just one. I just need one person to notice me.*

Immersed in his thoughts, his legs automatically propelled him past the street corner toward his studio apartment. An older gentleman sat on the sidewalk, his thin right arm outstretched and holding a small Styrofoam cup as Jayce walked by him.

"Now, I *know* he saw me," the gentleman said.

He was right, kind of. Jayce did look at him, but Jayce didn't *see* him. His mind was too occupied at that moment to really see anything or anyone. It was a good thing Jayce's legs worked on autopilot, or else he would've walked straight to Egypt before realizing where he was.

The gentleman had sadly grown accustomed to people giving him excuses, crossing to the other side of the sidewalk, averting their eyes away from him, or just flat out being rude to him. But not once had he seen someone look right into his eyes with absolutely no expression whatsoever. Now *that* was strange.

The gentleman watched Jayce walk away, wondering what in the world had just happened. It was in that moment that he decided he would rather have people purposely avoid him instead of looking right into his eyes with a blank expression like that.

"The thanks I get for serving this country," he sighed, referring to his service in the Vietnam War. "I guess no one cares about that anymore. All I did was risk my life every day for five years. But that's no big deal, right?"

A slight plop in his Styrofoam cup quickly shifted his attention. *Plop, plop. Plop, plop, plop.* A heavy rain announced its arrival. He silently braced himself for another long, sleepless night exposed to the cold rain. He hoped in his heart that this wouldn't make him get sick again.

He sighed, longing for a warm place to sleep, even for just one night. "I just wish someone would notice me."

The memory of this episode raced through my heart. I placed my paintbrush aside and decided to finish the sunset a bit later.

My oh my, we all desire to be noticed, don't we?

Buzz, buzz.

"Dad? There's someone here to see you. He doesn't want to talk to me; he insists on speaking only to you." As he spoke, a brisk, middle-aged man brushed past him and walked quickly to me. "Hi, me again," the man started. "I hate to bother you with this, but I really need a favor. A huge favor. I just—"

"Excuse me." I interrupted his vain repetitions. "Did you see who you just walked by?"

He turned around to see who I was referring to, his eyes landing on my son. "Oh, yes, I see him. As a matter of fact, I've heard of him before." He gave my son a quick wave. "Roger Cavers, nice to meet you." He immediately turned back to me and resumed his plea. "Like I was saying, I was wondering if you could—"

"How many kids do you have, Roger?"

"One," he responded, taken aback. "A little girl. And she sure is expensive! See, that's kinda why I'm here today. I need—"

"Do you have a house?"

"Well, yes, I do. And hopefully I'll be able to keep it if you do me a favor." Roger spoke with the candor and curtness of a seasoned car salesman. "If I don't get—"

"How would you feel if someone rushed into your house and completely ignored your daughter?"

"Well, uh, that would be, that would be kinda messed up, I guess. That would be kinda rude if ya asked me."

"You're right, Roger; it would be *kinda rude*. Now, how would you feel if that same person ignored your daughter *every* time they came to your house?"

"I wouldn't like it. No, I wouldn't like it at all." Visible confusion spread across Rogers' face. He glanced quickly at my son and then back at me. "Please, I don't know what all this is about, but I just—"

"Okay, now how would you like it if over the course of twenty-six years, that same person rushed into your house and completely ignored your daughter each time they came over?"

"I'm sorry, I'm so sorry. I just…. please forgive me. I've said nothing but nice things about your son. Honest, I really have. I've done a lot of good in my life, I've helped thousands of people with my business and—"

"Okay, so here's the thing, Roger. How you have treated my son is not how you would want someone to treat your daughter. And how you treat my son is how you treat me. As a parent I'm sure you can understand where I'm coming from, right?"

Roger now had a choice to make. He could focus on trying to get his needs met, or he could notice the one who really matters. What good parent would be okay with someone who kept treating their child as though they don't exist? Not me. And apparently not Roger either.

Whether first dates, business endeavors, or passersby on the street, everyone has a desire to be noticed. Valued. Loved. Including my son and me.

Table for One ... Again

"**S**o I'm just sitting there, and she's scrolling through her phone the whole time. The *whole* time!"

His words came out with the same frustration he had felt in that moment. His heart raced.

"Well, did she talk about anything at all? Did she even speak?" his dad inquired.

"Barely. It was like she couldn't bring herself to say anything to me. The few times she did speak to me, it felt so forced. I could tell she didn't want to be there. Every so often she would realize that it had been quiet for a few minutes, and she seemed like she kinda felt bad about being on her phone, so she would try to say something. Like: *You're so kind* and *Thank you for everything*. And that's how it went the entire time. She says she loves me all the time and that she wants to spend forever with me, but today she treated me like I was an afterthought."

His father had heard this story many times before. The scenarios were almost identical: someone would express interest in his son, tell him they wanted to spend time with him, and then not show up at all, or show up and be completely distracted to the point where his son felt like he was on a date by himself. It was an unfortunate sight, seeing it play out so many times with so many different people. No matter how often it happened, each time still hurt.

"If she wanted to spend time with me like she said she did, like she told everyone that she was going to, then why did she treat me like this when we finally got together? I mean, I could see if I were hard to get in touch with or something like that. But no, I made myself completely available like I always do. I'm here for her all the time. There's nothing more I could have done to let her know that I was there for her." He closed his eyes and breathed deeply. "She didn't even have to come to my house, Dad. We were just going to hang out in her room; she didn't even have to get dressed up and go anywhere."

A loud crack of thunder roared across the sky, echoing the passion of his voice.

He thought of all the times he had watched his lover become absolutely enraged whenever she got stood up or pushed to the side. Her usually quiet nature would do a complete 180 in a matter of seconds. She was super sensitive to those types of things because she always went out of her way to please others. So when the most minimal consideration was not given to her, she didn't take it well at all.

"And to think, this is the same person who hates being ignored. Imagine if I would have treated her the way she has treated others who've ignored her. But you know what, Dad? Even though I was not happy with the way things turned out, I won't treat her the way she treated me. I love her too much."

He placed his head in his scarred, powerful hands. Right on cue, the clouds below released torrents of rain. Several of those raindrops gracefully landed on the woman he had been speaking about. She looked up to the sky as she left her apartment, bracing herself for the oncoming rain.

"Ugh, I should've checked the weather this morning," she said to herself.

She covered her head with her jacket and hurried down the street. She didn't have time to go back for her umbrella. Her ex-boyfriend was waiting for her downtown, and she didn't want to be late.

Watching her as she ran down the street below, he continued speaking to his father. "I really wanted her to be present with me. There was so much I was going to tell her, Dad. Everything she had been crying about: her break up, the betrayal—everything. I was right there for her, but her mind was on everyone else except me."

His father embraced him. No words were exchanged. And as is par for the course whenever a warm embrace is involved, in comes the flood of all the memories that make the emotions much more vivid. He now began to think of all the times people were on the way to meet with him, but ended up getting so distracted with other people, hobbies, brunch dates, and football games that they never made it to him. In his mind he saw hordes of people headed toward him but never reaching the place where he was waiting for them. They got swept away in books, arguments, Taco Tuesdays, Netflix—everything but *him*. He sat and watched as they went on millions of detours that led them farther and farther away from him; one detour leading to another and then another. He would check in from time-to-time to see if they still wanted to see him, but he wouldn't force it. So he would simply knock, leaving it up to them to answer.

He made himself available every time. Every. Single. Time. He never cancelled, rescheduled at the last minute, stood anyone up—never. With each missed date, he thought of what could have been. They could have had a beautiful time together talking, laughing, falling deeper and deeper in love.

His father could relate to his pain. As a parent, whatever happens to your child, happens to you too. His father felt every canceled date, every excuse, every *Oh, I'm so sorry, but this is way more important than you right now* that was never spoken but said indirectly through repeated actions. He knew that his son always showed up on time with anticipation and waited and waited for each one of his loved ones to show up.

"This was supposed to be our time together. I was right there, ready. I know exactly how much time she has left, so that's why today was so important. Every day I try to get through to her," he said.

"I love you, son. I'll always be here for you. I'm not going anywhere any time soon." They smiled. "After all, you're a pretty great catch. You can literally give these people the world. Who wouldn't want to spend forever with you?"

"Thanks, Dad. I knew you would understand."

He stood up and stretched. Somewhere in the distance, the universe expanded a bit further too.

Looking down below, his father said, "Looks like she's heading back to her apartment. I'm sure she wants to talk to you now."

"Of course I'll be there for her," his son replied. "I'll be right there no matter what."

My Son's Room

As a parent, seeing your child in pain is never easy. It stirs up emotions in you that you didn't even know you had.

I walked with my friend to her son's room. Her son sat on the floor, crying uncontrollably. She sat down next to him and wrapped him in her arms. He had been bullied unmercifully every day for two months. Rumors had spread that his family had infected people with COVID-19. The kids refused to talk to him and even ran away from him in fear of catching the "Chinese Flu." The attacks had recently become physical; he was pushed and kicked when other kids felt he was standing too close to them. The rumors had even spread to social media. It had quickly gotten out of control, with harassing phone calls and threats.

I knew exactly how his mother felt and didn't want her to face this pain alone. So I went with her to her son's room, and I did what any good friend would do: I stayed by her side. I stayed with her in her grief. She wrapped her arms around her son, and I wrapped my arms around them both. There were no words exchanged, but I know my presence provided comfort.

As she looked down at her son, in her mind she saw him as a newborn in the NICU. He had been diagnosed with a rare heart condition and was writhing in her arms in pain, completely inconsolable. She tried her best to hold him firmly and comfort him at the same time, but the more she tried, the more he resisted. His constant twisting caused the IV in his nose to move, which painfully scraped his throat. He moved so much that she was no longer able to hold him and had to place him back in his incubator, which crushed her heart even more. Looking down at him now, she felt the same helplessness and pain in her heart that she had that day in the NICU.

To hold someone who doesn't want to be held, what a tragic story, one which I know all too well. The memory she had of her son reminded me of all the times I had held her as she writhed in my arms in pain, completely inconsolable. The more she resisted my hold on her, the more pain it caused her. Her pain stemmed from a spiritual heart condition, one that had been passed down through the generations, manifesting itself physically in her son.

Now it was time for her to walk with me to my son's room. I wanted to show her that I understood what she was going through, that I could relate to her pain, because my son had been bullied, mocked, beaten, tortured, falsely accused, and eventually murdered in cold blood. I wanted her to see what I did for her and her son, so that she could be comforted, loved, and healed.

But instead she stayed in her son's room, convincing herself that she was all alone. In her mind she was carrying this pain by herself. She refused to believe that I could truly love her if I allowed this to happen to her son. I wanted to show her otherwise, but she would have to come with me to my son's room to receive the truth.

For now I'll stay with her in her son's room until she comes with me to my son's room.

We Talked About You

"So let me get this straight; I basically have to leave home and go get treated like an enemy of the worst kind?" I asked.

"Well, yes."

"Okay, but you want me to do this for people who are *against* you?"

"Yes, that's correct."

"Okay, I need you to run this by me one more time, for clarity's sake," I said, already knowing in my heart what the answer would be.

After looking at me intently, He turned and faced Himself in the mirror. Then He began explaining everything to me again.

"I'm going to let certain people know that you're coming. So it's not going to be a surprise to them. Your cousin is getting people ready for you now as we speak. Just like I'm giving you the heads up, I'm preparing others for you too. But the thing is, just because you and the others know what's going to happen, that won't make it any easier. In fact there will be a time when you will come and ask me if I even want all this to happen.

"You will go, and you will be cared for by a family who will love you very much. But even their enormous amount of love for you won't keep them from misunderstanding you. Don't take it personally. One day soon they will understand you.

"You'll grow, take care of my business, gain wisdom and knowledge, and find favor with me and with others. You will be a blessing to others. After thirty years you will begin your ministry and face numerous challenges because of it. You will be accused, rejected, called names, and even kicked out of certain places. At one point people will even try to murder you, but you'll be able to walk right out of it.

"Your closest friends and relatives will disappoint you, but you will also do many amazing things that will change people's lives. You will heal them, teach them, love them, and bless them. People all over the world will know about you, even if they don't accept you. You're going to change the course of history.

"But you must understand that all this comes with a heavy price. You're not going to make it out alive."

He stopped for a moment to let His words sink into my heart and then continued. "In fact, you will experience the worst pain imaginable. You'll be arrested, falsely accused, forced to stand trial, and condemned to die by the same city that you performed miracles in. There will be crowds at your miracles, but only a handful will be there for you at the cross. You will be beaten unmercifully, almost to the point of death. You're going to hear the sound of your own flesh tearing. You will have to carry the entire weight of the world on your shoulders and walk through throngs of people who hate you. They're going to crucify you like a criminal and smile as your blood stains their hands. The nails that they place in your body will drain the blood out of you. It will be almost impossible for you to breathe.

"Even in this condition, you will still serve me. You'll pray for your murderers, you will make sure that your mother is cared for, and you'll also encourage one of the men being crucified alongside you. As blood pours down your face, you will look out and see people mocking you and condemning you. You'll hear your murderers casting lots for your clothes. Your dear mother will be there, full of grief. It will be extremely difficult for you to look at her, but she will be there to witness the entire ordeal.

"What they give you to drink at this time won't quench your thirst at all. In fact it will make it worse. There will be no comfort given to you whatsoever, so with all your might you will have to encourage yourself and remember why you are doing this. That is the only thing that is going to help you through this."

After a few moments, I asked the daunting question: "And this is the only way I can save them? Is there *any* other way?"

"This is the only way to save them. It has to be this way."

"And if I don't do this for them, what then? What would happen to them?"

"They won't make it," He said. "They'd have absolutely no way to get back to me. Without you there's no hope, no future for them at all. You are the best gift I can offer. Riches run out eventually, and fame can be corrupted. And anyone can give out material gifts, which can always be replaced or remade. There are many other options I could have chosen. But if I give them something that someone else can give them, or take credit for, then the whole message is lost. They wouldn't know how much I love them. Any other option would not express how much they mean to me. There's no denying my love if I'm willing to sacrifice my only son for them. That's why I'm sending you."

I considered everything He had said during our conversations—the joys, the sorrows, the unbearable pain. It was a lot to process. I appreciated being able to know what was up ahead; after all, a good father fully prepares his son for the good and the bad, even when it's hard. But being prepared still wouldn't make this process any easier for me. I was being sent to lose absolutely everything and to suffer terribly along the way.

But then I thought of you.

I remembered how much I loved you, and I knew how much you needed me. The only way you could live is if I died. And not only did I have to die, but I had to die a slow, agonizing death. However, if I went through with this, you would be saved, and then we could be together forever.

My heart stirred. My mind was made up. Even if you were the only one I had to go through all this for, I would still do it.

"I'll go. Whatever it takes, I'll do it. I *have* to do it. I'm in love."

Still looking at Himself in the mirror, He smiled. In the blink of an eye, I became His reflection in the mirror. We embraced one last time before I left.

"I love you," I said.

"I love you, more," came His honest reply.

But I Bled for You

My precious daughter looked down at me and said, "No, I won't do it. I will never forgive them."

Her words ripped through my heart. I looked up at her, and all I could see was red. Not red because of the anger her words carried, but red because of the physical pain that coursed through my head. My breaths became shorter. My body was weakened from copious amounts of anguish. I struggled to simply lift my head, but I badly wanted to behold my child, to see her face, her expression, because surely this wasn't happening. Surely she wasn't turning her back on me. Surely she wasn't about to walk away and never return.

With all the strength I could muster, I lifted myself onto my left elbow. Resting my weight on it was excruciating, but other options were unavailable at the moment. I imagined how I looked to her: sprawled out on the floor, broken, barely breathing. The sight of me in this diminished state would evoke compassion from the coldest heart, but hers seemed unmovable. Did she remember all the compassion I had shown her? All the understanding and comfort that I had given her? I couldn't tell which one hurt more: the words she had said or the fact that she was serious about saying them.

My right hand reached out to her. For a second, it seemed as though she would change her mind. Perhaps it was only wishful thinking, but there seemed to be a hesitance, an uncertainty in her eyes. We had never been in this place together before. There was no precedent in our history together for what was now taking place. Her entire eternity would rest on what she did next. Almost as if on cue, her cold stare returned, and the light I had hoped for, if it was ever there, quickly left her eyes.

"No."

My arm dropped to the floor, and soon enough I was on my back again. My head throbbed. Her response drained the life out of the place in my heart that was strictly for her. I had wanted to keep looking at her, to keep searching her eyes, but her no had pushed me out of her life, out of her eternity. Her subsequent footsteps echoed further and further away, each one cutting me deeply because I knew where she was headed.

The blood from my temple began making its way toward the back of my head before falling to the ground in rapid drops. Her *no* had stretched every gash and tear on my body one inch wider. The meat of my back stuck to the ground under me in a sickeningly sweet embrace, cementing my position with flesh. My scars now glued me to the ground, promising to rip me again if I had the audacity to lift myself up.

"But...I bled for you."

My mouth continued to echo this cry of my heart.

"I bled for you."

"I bled for you."

"I bled for you."

"My love...I bled for you."

Only silence and pain followed.

I reached out for her again. I could see her form in the distance through the hole in my hand.

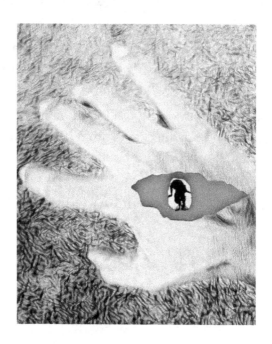

My head began to feel tight, and my mouth had become a desert. My legs found no bearable position because as soon as my torn skin touched the ground, searing pain shot through my limbs and raced to my heart. The toll that even the slightest movement took on my ripped back was too great, yet I desperately wanted to keep my battered skin from touching the ground. This was the misery of being too hurt to even writhe in pain.

The hand I had used to reach for her was now circled in a pool of blood next to me. My face burned as my tears fought violently with the fresh scratches on my face. I shivered with fevers of an unknown origin, sensing the onset of infection in every one of my limbs. My stomach churned with sadness, hunger, and sickness. This was the cruelest rejection imaginable, and who knew it would be at the hands of the one that I love.

She saw what her *no* did to me, and my resulting pain wasn't enough to change her mind. My beloved saw me broken, and her only response was: *No, I won't forgive them.*

All I had done was love her. All I had done was save her life, dragging the death angel away from her door night after night. All I had done was give her my life. And what I had asked her to do was forgive those who had hurt her.

"I bled for you," I whispered to ears that would now forever be closed to me.

Part II

WHAT WE DO WITH HIS LOVE

Five Minutes

"You said all that to say …?" With his frustration growing, he motioned with his hands for me to basically spit it out already.

"I just think that the process would be more efficient if we modified the outputs, that's all."

There. I spat it out.

"Okay, but how can we guarantee that?" He peered at me over his glasses. "We have to back up any changes we make. You *do* know that, right?"

Thank God for a great poker face because my eyes were begging to roll to the back of my head. I had just explained this to him. He clearly hadn't been listening.

"One idea is to subcontract the construction to one of our vendors, which would give our team more time to focus on restructuring the processes on the front end. Essentially two teams would be working simultaneously, finish at around the same time, and then we could roll out—"

"But don't you know how much that would cost? We can't fund something like this right now!"

Yet another sign that he hadn't been listening at all. Funding was the first thing I talked about as he rushed me into his office, announcing his perpetual *I've only got five minutes* spiel.

"Well, with the new grant—"

"Grant? What grant? Who has a grant?"

The one you signed off on last week. "The technical assistance grant from—"

"Oh yeah, yeah, yeah, yeah," he said as he resumed scrolling through his phone.

"So like I was saying, the grant would cover just the type of work we'd be doing, which is operational change, and I think—"

"Ugh! I hate when she does this!"

His outburst made me jump back in my seat. He had clearly tuned me all the way out at this point. He wasn't even trying to act interested in our conversation anymore. *Thanks for rushing me in here just to ignore me, boss.*

But I had worked hard just to get some time with him. I was frustrated, but I wasn't about to blow my one chance. He needed to hear what I had to say.

Pushing past my frustration and corporate pleasantries, I said, "Sir, if you could please allow me to——"

"Look, I appreciate your consideration, I really do." He stood to collect his coat. "But I just don't have time right now. I've gotta run. You'll have to circle back to me on this, but to be honest with you, I don't think it's gonna work."

So he basically ignored me, rushed me, and still didn't consider what I had to say. And to make matters worse, I would now have to work extra hard to dig this company out of an oncoming mess we could have avoided if he'd just taken my advice.

Happy Monday.

***

I was off—finally. I just needed to squeeze in a prayer so I could kick back the rest of the night. It had been a rough one.

"So yeah, I've had so much going on lately. I really need to get it together. But I wanted you to know I appreciate you, and thank you for being so patient with me while I've been slacking. I'm just so annoyed with the way things are going at work. I hate feeling like I'm not being listened to. That triggers me like no other. I don't think I'm the best account exec by a long shot, but I have come up with some good ideas. It's just that no one ever listens, and it's so frustrating.

"But yeah, I'll listen to that devotional you told me about though. Thank you so much. I love you."

Okay, okay. Everything was good. I felt much better. Prayer always worked.

As I searched for my remote, I heard someone behind me say, "So I only get five minutes too?"

Turning around, of course I saw no one because I'd lived alone for the past eleven years. *What the world?*

I was definitely exhausted, but this was some next-level exhaustion because I'd never heard anything so clearly before. Replaying what I heard in my head, I continued searching for my remote, occasionally glancing behind me, you know, just in case. I made a mental note of where my gun was stored and began to relax. I just needed to chill out.

But I couldn't. The question seemed so on point. I was still frustrated by the meager five minutes I was given to make my pitch at work today, so it was pretty obvious that this had something to do with that. But who—

Oh, of course. I get it now.

I'd been complaining about being rushed and ignored this whole time. For months, even. And what do I do? Treat God the exact same way. I talk to Him, but I hadn't listened to Him at all. My God.

Sitting back down, my head naturally found my hands. The remote was on the floor in between my feet, in plain sight even though I couldn't find it earlier. God was even gracious enough to make sure I didn't get distracted with the show I had planned to watch. That's how much He wanted my attention. And I only gave Him five minutes of a twenty-four-hour day.

"I am so, so sorry. I don't even know what to say." My heart pounded in my chest, and I didn't dare try to wipe the tears that began to flow. "I'm just so sorry."

My heart hurt because I could now see how He felt. I had been treating Him the way that I hated being treated, and there was no justification whatsoever.

"I'm here," He soothed me with just two words. "We can talk if you'd like. I've got all the time in the world. Literally."

Another One

Another one.

Another one.

And another one.

~DJ Khaled

"Sure thing, I'll take care of it." Lakiesha scribbled a few notes in her agenda, writing small so that she could squeeze it in between lines of pre-existing tasks.

"Unfortunately, this can't wait," her manager, Affion, said politely but curtly. "We're already way behind schedule, so we've got to play catch up at this point. The whole world is coming back to life again, and we have to be ready." He slid another file across the table then stood up. "Any questions? I've got a hard stop—like now, though."

Lakiesha also rose from her seat. "Real quick; when do I need to have all this done?"

"Immediately. Absolutely no delays. I'm counting on you." He headed for the door. "You're the only one who can get this done. Don't let me down."

Lakiesha began to collect the rest of her work. As she stacked the files one on top of the other, the pile began to teeter to one side. She caught it with both hands, trying her best to steady the leaning tower of work. She decided to just guide the pile over to one side to stop it from spilling everywhere, and from there she split the pile into two. She sat down again and began sifting through them.

"I may as well organize them now since I gotta go through them all anyway," she mumbled.

With a deep breath, she picked up one file and opened it. After a few moments, she noticed she had been staring blankly at the first page for five minutes. *C'mon, think, Kiesha, think.* She readjusted herself in the chair and leaned in closer to her work, as if that would help. It definitely did not help. Her posture made her look focused, but her mind was still somewhere else.

For starters Affion only remembered her when there was an emergency. Before he could thank her for one task, he came in with even more requests. Everything with him was always urgent, super urgent. But Lakiesha dutifully carried out each assignment as best she could. She was your typical overworked and severely under-appreciated associate.

But now sitting in an empty conference room with a slippery slope of urgent work, she began to wonder exactly why she was doing this. She had been with the company for years, and after all this time it seemed as if no one cared about her.

I'm not going to get any acknowledgment, any pay raise, any consideration. My thank you will be another pile of work! No one ever asks me how I'm doing—ever. They treat me like a machine, and I'm actually starting to feel like one. That's nothing to look forward to.

I sure wish emergencies weren't the only time they remembered me.

***

I began to picture all of the urgent requests that Lakiesha had sent me. I thought of all the times she had come to me with these requests, remembering each instance in vivid detail. When her mother got sick, when her car got stolen, whenever her job got stressful ... those seemed to be the only times she reached out to me.

But I came through every time—on time—just as she expected me to. She had yet to ask me how I felt or if I wanted anything from her. But the second she thought I was late or not answering her, she'd stop speaking to me altogether.

I sure wish that emergencies weren't the only time she remembered me.

Comrades and Captives

*T*he carnage was unreal. Bodies were strewn everywhere, still twisted into the positions they were in as they took their last breath. Some had been running toward the enemy's camp, some had been hiding, and some looked as though they had simply fallen asleep where they were. Death had forever frozen their bodies in the middle of their last act.

I walked through the battlefield with my comrade Darius. I watched his eyes scan the ghastly scene around us. I wrapped my arm around his shoulders.

"Just breathe, take it easy."

Scores of our other comrades buzzed quickly around us, some trying to revive soldiers lying on the ground, some rushing toward the frontline, some literally dragging their comrades out of dangerous territory. There was movement in every direction as we had all been called to fight. Only the dead stood still.

War raged around us. Every now and then an enemy combatant slipped into our territory and meticulously kidnapped one of our own. It would happen so quickly and subtly that it would have gone unnoticed but for the shrieks of triumph from the captor or the screams of terror from the captive. On occasion one of our comrades would be rescued and moments later end up in a tug-of-war to rescue someone else.

Out of nowhere a sharp *swoosh* broke past us as a comrade in front of us was snatched by an enemy combatant. Darius charged toward the pair, running as fast as his legs would carry him.

"Hey!" he screamed at the top of his lungs. "It's your fault; this is all your fault!"

He continued running after them, trampling carelessly over bodies and other injured comrades who were no longer able to fight. Some of the ones he raced past reached out, hoping Darius would help them up, but his mind was focused ahead.

"You should've listened to me. I told you not to do it. I told you. You knew better. Now look at you!"

Darius hurled his words not at the enemy combatant but at the one who had been kidnapped. His pace slowed as he began to lose his speed, the enemy disappearing into the distance with our comrade. Darius stopped and bent over, placing his hands on his knees to catch his breath. Head bowed, his chest heaved deeply with each breath. A trembling arm profusely dripping blood reached out to him from below. Darius glanced down in disgust at one of our bruised and bloodied comrades.

"I don't have time," he snarled, pushing the outstretched arm away from him. "Take care of yourself."

Darius began walking back toward me, his eyes red with fury. "I cannot believe he didn't listen to me. I'm not even surprised he got kidnapped. He had it comin' to him." I was tending to another one of our comrades as Darius approached. "What are you doing?" Darius asked in surprise.

"This is what I came here to do. To help."

"Yeah, but ..." Darius was distracted by yet another kidnap. "Good God, I know him too. Jesse!"

His hands tied, Jesse walked slowly, his shoulders slumped, his head down as the enemy combatant led him away. Darius ran to catch up with his old friend, then shoved him from behind.

"Jesse, I can't believe this. You're really this weak, huh? You're better than this! Now look at you. Pathetic!"

Jesse and his captor continued their slow march across the battlefield. Darius stopped and turned back toward me, throwing his hands in the air. "Unbelievable!"

Just then another comrade swooped in and began fighting Jesse's captor, viciously attacking him until he dropped the rope that bound Jesse. The comrade then grabbed Jesse by the arm and ran full speed with him in the opposite direction. I rejoiced.

Darius eventually made his way back to me, and we later continued walking. As the night drew closer, the battle intensified, as the enemy tended to increase his attacks at night. Right before nightfall, we saw a large iron crate in the middle of our path. As we came closer, we saw one of our female comrades lying on the floor of the crate, barely moving. Darius reached to open the gate, and as he did the woman startled awake. Lifting her head, her swollen eyes and battered face became visible. Scars covered almost every inch of her body, and the parts of her that were hidden by her torn uniform were equally scarred. Darius opened the gate wide and took a step inside. The woman watched his every move, her eyes wide and somber.

Once she noticed that the pattern on his uniform was the same as hers, her face relaxed. She reached her hand out to him. In one fell swoop Darius grabbed her wrist before she could touch him.

"Don't you dare touch me," he snarled. "You deserve to be here."

Throwing her hand to the side, he marched out of the crate and slammed the door shut. Using a crowbar that had been lying on the ground, he sealed the door shut so that she couldn't escape. The woman ran to the door after seeing what he had done. She dropped to her knees, crying as she pulled at the door.

"No, God, no!"

Darius stormed off, ignoring her screams. I took the crowbar and pried the door of the crate open. The woman ran to me, and I cradled her in my arms as she cried. It had taken Darius more energy to lock her in the crate than it would've taken him to simply open it and care for her as I had done.

Watching Darius walk away, I recalled all the marching orders I had given him preparing for battle. We had spent years together, and he had worked hard to excel in his training. Yet almost as soon as he had been promoted and given some authority, Darius had not only gone against his orders and everything he had been taught, but all sense of morality had left him as well. He had essentially become a traitor, betraying his fellow comrades by allowing them to be taken captive, refusing to tend to their injuries, and leaving them stranded. Though Darius was on my side, he was fighting against me as he refused to help rescue our captive comrades. Comrades who were not rescued were more than likely to join the enemy's side at some point, which would make our work even harder. But Darius refused to see the bigger picture.

Before reaching the battlefield, Darius had constantly boasted about his relationship with me, reminding everyone of his past promotions and achievements. But the battle we were currently in revealed that he didn't truly have the heart of a soldier. While treating his fellow comrades mercilessly, he talked and confided in me as if he had done no wrong, even regularly asking me for favor. But I saw and heard absolutely everything he did on the battlefield, repeatedly breaking the golden rules of combat: defeat the enemy, help your fallen comrades, and leave no one behind.

Yet Darius still expected to win because of his own strength and knowledge. He behaved this way because he believed that all the good things he did would push him to victory. After all, he did attack the enemy head-on and worked to train others in battle techniques. And yes, this work is very important in defeating the enemy.

But what good is it if you fight the enemy then turn around and make it easier for the enemy to win?

Brethren, if a man is overtaken in any trespass, you who are spiritual restore such a one in a spirit of gentleness, considering yourself lest you also be tempted. Bear one another's burdens, and so fulfill the law of Christ.

Galatians 6:1-2

Just a Sip

Just one more sip. One more sip won't hurt.

Trudy was shaking nervously, slumped in a small pile on the floor, hands wrapped tightly around her knees. Cold sweat seeped through her blouse and poured from her temple, smearing her mascara and lipstick. She pulled herself off the floor and crawled slowly to her bedroom.

Dragging her knees across the floor, a sense of excitement began building in her. After trying to talk herself out of it for the good part of an hour, Trudy was finally letting go and doing what she wanted to do.

Everyone needs to satisfy their cravings once in a while. I deserve it.

Her pace picked up as she neared her bedroom door. Once over the threshold, she paused. Still on all fours she could see the glorious bottle on her dresser. It stood tall amidst her array of perfumes, lotions, and make-up brushes. In one unsteady motion she stood to her feet and ran toward her dresser. She had no hesitation reaching for the bottle. The swift motion made her lose balance, and she quickly grabbed her dresser with her free hand.

Easy there, girl.

There seemed to always be something inside for her, no matter how much she drank—excuse me, *sipped*, since according to her she was *not* a drinker. She had convinced herself that one sip every now and again was enough to help keep her sane. With one deep, satisfying breath, she took a slow sip of her heart's delight.

"Cheers to my second wind."

Trudy's eyes closed as she thought of everything that she wanted to do with this second wind: trips to plan, people to call, children to raise.

Now that I'm in control, I can handle all this.

Opening her eyes, she studied the bottle held tightly in her hand. "Until next time."

A sudden sadness came over her, as though she were bidding farewell to a dear friend. She had purposely held off today, trying desperately to convince herself that she didn't need it.

But we both know that's a lie, don't we?

Out of nowhere, she was suddenly unable to leave the place where she stood. She looked up at herself in the mirror. Straightening her shoulders, she gripped the bottle even tighter.

That's it; I'm done playing games. I need it, and it's fine. I could be doing much worse things. There's nothing wrong with controlling my own life!

"How 'bout you come with me this time? That would make things a lot easier, don't you think?" She promptly placed the bottle in her purse. "There. Perfect."

Without missing a beat, she resumed what she had been doing before she began fighting the urge not to drink—sip—that had left her huddled on the floor for an hour. She promptly washed her face, reapplied her makeup, and changed her clothes.

Shoes, mask, phone. Good to go.

She left her condo and walked briskly down the street to pick up her children. As she walked, the bottle sat neatly in her purse, clanking gently against her keys with each step. Knowing it was there and being able to hear it put her mind at ease.

As if checking in on a baby in a stroller, she peeked into her purse while standing at the crosswalk. Peering inside she could see the bottle's label written in bold letters.

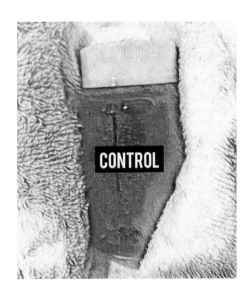

She smiled. *I couldn't do this without you.*

Time Is My Essence

*I*n the spirit realm Jovan was drooling over his watch again. He bowed down and worshipped it in an eerily ritualistic manner.

"My time is too valuable to waste. My time is too valuable to waste."

This was the incessant chant he offered to the idols of time. He brought every one of his relationships to the altar as a sacrifice. The idols he worshipped received his precious care, his money, and his attention.

In the natural Jovan was reviewing his schedule for the day, which was perfectly laid out. The thought of being productive with his every waking moment made him feel alive. *Time waits for no man, and neither will I.* This was a hard-learned lesson gleaned from his father's early death.

Jovan set his alarms for the day while brushing his teeth. *Alarms are such a great way to wrap things up. People can be so long-winded, but a quick chirp from the alarm always shuts them up.* He smirked. *You can't argue with time.*

10:00 haircut

10:45 meeting

11:30 meeting

12:30 lunch meeting

1:15 submit draft proposal

1:30 conference call

2:00 staff interviews

3:30 conference call

4:00 client follow up calls

4:45 pick up kids

6:00 dinner

Today's schedule was more or less the same as every other day. Meetings, calls, and other important Corporate America activities. Jovan was the go-to guy, the one who got things done. He prided himself on multitasking, considering it a skill he'd mastered over the years.

"The more efficient you become, the more you can get done," he always said.

After all, he worked in a super-competitive industry, so one slip up could affect the good money he made. Yes, it grew tiring at times, and every day was stressful, but Jovan knew that stress came with the territory of success. His father always taught him to do his best and never give up, no matter what.

Being a good father was very important to Jovan, so he always made time for his family. That was one of the main reasons why he scheduled his days to ensure he had the evenings free for his wife and children. Ignoring comments about being a workaholic, Jovan concluded that those types of people never made time for anything other than work, and he was not like that because he specifically set aside time for his family.

In the spirit realm Jovan was sitting Indian style on the floor, watching a movie roll filled with different headlines. His expression was like that of a child captivated by his favorite cartoon, his eyes wide with wonder. The idols of time stood over him, fiercely pushing away his awareness, his calmness, his peace. In the natural Jovan was sitting in the barber's chair, casually responding to emails, and sending text messages.

His barber was used to Jovan's hunched over posture, gently tilting his head back whenever he leaned too far forward to read his phone. It was annoying, but Jovan tipped well, so it wasn't that big of a deal. Plus his barber needed all the tips he could get as recent hospital visits had torn a huge hole in his pocket. Before getting up to leave, Jovan slipped his earphones in and listened to his favorite podcast on current events.

"There's no reason anyone should be clueless as to what's going on in the world," he often told his wife. "Information is free and readily available; people just don't take the time to inform themselves."

Fully updated, Jovan walked into his first meeting of the day, cracking a joke to his colleagues about one of the current events he had just listened to on his way to the office. He poured himself some coffee as he continued his chatter, grabbing a cereal bar for breakfast and taking his seat.

Three minutes to chat and eat, not too shabby.

As the clock stroke 10:45, he called the meeting to order and began his presentation.

"Excellent presentation, Jovan," Mr. Mensah told him after the meeting.

"Just trying to be like you, Mr. Mensah!"

The congratulations from his boss gave him butterflies. He remembered how he had set aside time to prepare and rehearse his presentation, and a deep sense of pride entered his heart for his time management.

In the spirit realm Jovan was racing on a treadmill-like device, reaching out to clocks of diverse shapes and sizes in an attempt to grab at least one. They were all just beyond his reach, which made him try harder and harder. He raced and raced, trying desperately to grab the idols of time. In the natural Jovan was hurrying to his office, trying to avoid his assistant Jan, who he assumed had a flurry of follow-up questions about his presentation. She quickly approached him, but Jovan had only seven minutes until his next meeting.

"Jan, shoot me an email. I've gotta prep for the Ngozi meeting. Can you bring them to the conference room? They're probably already here. Thanks!"

He appreciated Jan, but her questions were always too many and too inconvenient. He was gently trying to train her how to follow up via email or text so that he could respond at his convenience, not just when she wanted an answer from him. He figured he was doing her a huge favor as most of his colleagues weren't as patient with their assistants. Jovan was firm, but he refused to condescend or be rude to anyone under him. There was no need for that. He preferred patience, positive reinforcement, and targeted hints to get his point across.

Jan watched Jovan hurry to his office to do his usual meeting prep routine: flip through notes too fast to even read them, check himself out in the mirror, pop in a breath mint, and check his emails for any last-minute cancellations. She sighed. *I guess I'll have to ask him for some time off a little later.*

She forced a smile and went to the reception area to greet the Ngozi representatives.

Just like clockwork, Jovan's stomach started to growl at 11:15.

Even my stomach is on schedule.

He smiled and continued his daydream. The Ngozi representatives were droning on and on about how their multimillion-dollar company couldn't fathom the idea of investing $300,000 in a new initiative that blah, blah, blah, blah, blah. Jovan nodded and agreed through the whole meeting while secretly planning his next course of action for these clients.

They're totally beating around the bush. I'll indulge them this time, but next time they're getting an ultimatum, then I'll ignore them for a few weeks before sending a final offer to close the deal. Gotta make 'em sweat a little.

"I totally understand," Jovan said as he shook hands with each representative and walked them to the reception area. "Especially in this investment climate, you can never be too sure. Maybe we'll have a miracle before our next meeting, and then we can go from there."

His fake consideration cracked him up. *Corny jokes and all, I'm gonna get them to cut the check.*

Jovan continued multitasking during his final tasks of the day, managing to mark every item off his to-do list. He packed his briefcase and headed for the door.

"And that, my friends, is how you get the job done," he announced to his office furniture.

Each day that went according to schedule further convinced Jovan that managing his time wisely was truly the key to his success. As long as he had everything under control and gave everything the exact amount of time he thought it needed, it would all work out fine. He often told his friends and colleagues that failure was a product of poor time management, not a lack of intellect.

Jovan picked his kids up from school five minutes ahead of schedule, waving to their teachers and making small talk with other parents along the way. He had just enough time to catch up with his kids, purposely turning off his radio so that he could engage them and hear about their day. He truly loved his children and felt blessed to be their father. Hearing their squeals and chatter made rush hour traffic bearable, and most importantly it was a great way to kill two birds with one stone: they didn't have to worry about being bullied on the school bus, and it gave them a chance to talk.

Walking in the house at 5:57, Jovan announced, "Honey, I'm home!"

Not one hiccup today, and I made it on time for dinner.

Closing out the day on such a high note was an adrenaline rush for him. Three years earlier Jovan and his wife had a huge blowout regarding his work schedule and the need for him *to actually be present* whenever he was home. Since then dinnertime had been set sharply at six o'clock, no excuses. That was when Jovan hired his assistant Jan and made it happen. He was still just as busy as he had been before, but he now managed his time differently so that he could be physically and mentally present with his family. His wife loved the change, and she could see the positive impact it made on the family.

In the spirit realm Jovan was slumped down in a metal chair, dozing off every few seconds, his head dropping to the side. He kept being rudely awakened by the sharp prod of an evil warlock. He struggled to stay awake, despite his exhaustion.

"Wake up!" the warlock screamed at him. "Think! Keep your mind running!"

In the natural Jovan lay in bed with his wife, his mind racing with his plans for tomorrow. He had much to do before the end of the week, and he wanted to be strategic about how to meet all his deadlines. His quiet time, when his wife was asleep, was usually when he reviewed his schedule for the next day, making minor tweaks as needed. For some reason it was a bit harder for him to focus tonight.

Although ideas continued to flood his tired mind, his thoughts kept drifting back to his barber. Jovan tried to remember if he had seen him wearing a hospital bracelet or not. He wasn't sure why this important detail even mattered, but it was one of those things where he couldn't really rest until he had an answer. He hated not knowing something. For a brief moment as he paid for his haircut, Jovan was certain he had seen a white hospital band on the barber's right wrist. He was an older gentleman, so if he was getting sick, Jovan wanted to know. He had been going to this same barber for years.

Isn't it bad that I don't know if the old man who cuts my hair is sick?

Jovan made a mental note to actually talk to his barber the next time he got a haircut. After deciding to do this, his thoughts continued leading him to other memories. He would have much rather resumed his mental preparations for tomorrow, but his thoughts seemed to demand a shift elsewhere. He began to think of the times where he was in his car, going at least 20 miles per hour over the speed limit so that he wouldn't be late for work or some other event. He also thought of the times when he got out of character because of someone else's tardiness or forgetfulness. *I just hate when people waste my time* was his go-to excuse. Picturing himself in those moments now made Jovan begin to reevaluate himself.

That night Jovan dreamed about Jan. He saw her in her office crying uncontrollably, with her back turned to the door. In her lap was an old, tattered dress that she held to her face as she cried. Jovan had never seen Jan like this before, and in his dream, he was at a loss for words. She cried and cried, not once looking up or turning to face him. Her cries made Jovan uncomfortable. He continued to stand in the doorway, watching Jan's shoulders heave with each sob.

Jan cried until Jovan woke up. It was 3:03 a.m. He still had another four hours and fifty-seven minutes to sleep, but he lay awake until his time left to sleep dwindled to three hours and then to two. He had a strange sense that the people around him had been crying out for help, and he had been completely oblivious.

In the spirit realm the idols of time paced nervously as they watched Jovan's attention shift away from them. They screamed and yelled at each other as they watched Jovan intently, doing their best to regain his attention. In the natural Jovan turned and watched his wife sleep. She looked so peaceful.

Is she hiding something from me again?

Their argument three years ago about dinner time was the last huge blowout they'd had, but what bothered him the most was finding out that she had felt that way for years. He remembered feeling so shocked that she had never said anything about it before. He had been under the impression that everything was completely fine.

What if there is something else she is holding back, and I've just been ignoring it?

Sleep-deprived, Jovan began his daily routine at a much slower pace than normal. He couldn't get his barber or Jan out of his mind. So strong was his conviction that he needed to speak with both of them that day, he made it a point to do so, even though he had not scheduled time for it.

After speaking with them he discovered that his barber had been diagnosed with pancreatic cancer, and Jan had been struggling with suicidal thoughts since the recent passing of her grandmother, who had raised her. Jovan was completely devastated. His heart broke for them, but he was also disgusted with himself for not having enough time in his day to simply notice them.

Something's gotta give, he thought as he watched Jan pack up for her bereavement leave. *Am I that in love with my schedule that I can't see people literally dying in front of me? Jesus. I know people worship things like cars and money, but here I am, worshipping time.*

In the spirit realm his idols gnashed their teeth, running wildly to hide behind unforgiveness, gluttony, and pride. Their imminent exposure was pure agony, and they howled in despair. Taking cover behind other vices was their first line of defense as this made it harder for them to be detected. In the natural Jovan felt a sharp pang in his head, almost as if he had been punched. He hated the fact that it took other people's suffering to make him realize the error of his ways. As he considered the hundreds of people he talked to, passed by on the street, and saw on a monthly basis, he began to wonder how many other things he had missed due to his strict adherence to his schedule.

I'm a nice person for sure, but am I a caring *person?*

Later that day an idea popped into his head. *I need to make time to* have *time for others.*

Being so consumed with scheduling, punctuality, and efficiency, Jovan ended up having no time left to give consideration to those around him. He never had time to just *be* because he always had a to-do list to keep up with. Absent an extreme emergency, Jovan bypassed whatever was not already planned ahead, and he didn't give it a second thought.

"That stops today. If me being efficient doesn't allow me to be a caring person, then what's the point?"

With his ever-so logical mind, Jovan began to write out his new plan to make time to have time:

Strike up a conversation with at least one stranger per day, and don't rush through it.

Do not pack your days with back-to-back activities. Give yourself extra time for each task just in case they run longer than expected, so you won't have to rush from one thing to the next in frustration.

Every Tuesday give one friend or relative a phone call just to see how they're doing.

Take your wife on a date every week—no excuses.

Enjoy quiet time at least once per day with no music, TV, or conversations. Just be quiet.

Identify what must be done each day (i.e., something with a specific deadline) as opposed to what you *want* to get done each day. Prioritize the musts and take care of the wants on an as-needed basis. It's okay if not everything gets done in one day.

Remember: you control your time; your time does not control you.

Most importantly, ask God what you should do with the time He has given you. *Lord, before I start my day, let me first start with you.*

"Well, this is a good place to start," Jovan said as he finished writing the last point. He liked that he was still able to use his skill set of planning ahead in a better, godlier way.

After years of sticking to strict schedules and timeframes, Jovan surprisingly felt very good about this new shift in his mindset. The idols of time, on the other hand, absolutely hated it. They coordinated daily and worked overtime and weekends to enslave him again. Sometimes they were successful in regaining his attention, but for the most part, Jovan was determined to stick it out and do what he knew was best. He understood that gaining a completely new mindset was not an overnight process, so he exercised patience with himself whenever he felt the urge to go back to his old ways. Deep down, he was proud of himself for recognizing and confronting one of the most hidden, subtle obsessions a person could have.

Glancing over at his schedule, he beamed with pride. "Time, you can run out but you can't run me!"

The Spot

"**I**t's a code blue, boss. Her blood pressure is through the roof. Her history of panic attacks complicates matters. She needs—"

"I actually know just what she needs," Luke's physician said.

"Okay," Luke continued, a bit confused. "Well, uh, so yeah, I was going to work to clear her arteries and get her blood pressure returned to normal. And the severe migraines—"

"Look, Dr. Oz," his physician quipped, then turned serious, "I need you to see the bigger picture. Do you know why this woman is really here?"

Now Luke was beyond confused. And to make matters worse, time didn't really allow for people in his profession to be confused, especially in the midst of a global pandemic. He was racing against the clock to save someone's life, yet he found himself trying to understand his own physician.

"I'm sorry, maybe I'm missing something." The silence that followed literally pushed Luke to continue talking. "So, yeah. She's here because she's showing signs of a stress-induced stroke, and if her situation doesn't change, she may never be the same again."

Even more silence.

This can't be good, Luke thought. He valued his physician and understood his ways—well, for the most part—but he couldn't stand the silent treatment. "Can you help me out? Help me understand? I'm sorry, I just can't figure out what you mean."

"For starters, you can ask me what I want you to do, instead of telling me what you're going to do. It'll help if you remember why I gave you this job in the first place. You wanted to go to art school, and you fought me tooth and nail on that until you finally gave in. I would hope by now you would see why I wanted you here."

Luke's thoughts raced full speed through his mind. *We really don't have time for thi—*

"Oh, don't worry," his physician said. "We have time. So like I was saying, I wanted you here for a reason, remember?"

"Yes, sir." Luke was a bit embarrassed and still 100 percent confused. By then he was too scared to even think to himself. So he just listened, silently praying that the answer he needed would come.

"Yes, she's in ER. Yes, she's code blue. Yes, her life is on the line. Long story short, because I know you're just *so* busy doing what I've told you to do and allowed you to do Dr. Oz," he teased, making Luke smile at his new nickname. "I wanted to tell you what her real problem is. She belongs to me after all. I was actually headed somewhere else but I heard you call me so I came here. And I *love* that you came to me for help. You told me about her, and you told me what you were planning to do to help her. But you haven't asked me what is it that I want for her."

That realization caused Luke to search deep inside himself. His mind raced back to the moment when he first saw the woman. Stress had sent her blood pressure through the roof, landing her in an overly-packed hospital. Luke learned her name when he saw her husband running behind the stretcher as they took her to the ICU.

"Samiyah! Samiyah!"

After that Luke's mind went into automatic survival mode. He could barely remember anything he had done in the operating room. He was just going by pure instinct at that point. He hadn't slept well since the outbreak and had barely eaten anything that day, so he was fueled only by adrenaline and a few sips of coffee.

With his hands moving robotically from Samiyah to the syringes to the machines, Luke prayed: *God, please let her make it back to her family. Please let her make it.*

Suddenly Luke was back in the empty breakroom by himself, his flashback officially over. "You there?" he asked.

"Welcome back, son. I'm still here."

"I prayed for her. I asked you to let her go back to her family because I didn't want her to die. But you're right; I never asked what *you* wanted to happen. It was an emergency, so I just figured that her life needed to be saved."

"And what did I tell you?"

Luke practically forced himself to remember. He pushed through the fatigue, the pain in his back, and the hole in his heart from his mother's recent diagnosis. This was hard. He looked out of the window at the 2:39 a.m. sky, his exhausted eyes searching the clouds as if to catch a glimpse of his physician.

"You said she's not waking up," Luke whispered.

"Yes, that's what I said. Son, I get that you're tired, stressed, afraid. You may have forgotten, but I did answer you. I always answer you, even when it's not the answer you want to hear."

"I'm sorry. I really am."

"I know. I am so pleased that you took the time to let me walk you through this because it's not about you or Samiyah. It's about me. Sometimes you get caught up in the circumstances, and naturally there is always a pull to pray that someone is healed so they can live. I get it. But you have to remember that I view things from the perspective of eternity, so living here on Earth is not always going to be my will. Before Samiyah was even born, I knew exactly what day she would come back to me. So no, she's not going to wake up here, but she *is* going to wake up with me, which is much better than her waking up on this side. And not only will she wake up, but because she'll be with me, she won't be sick anymore. Or ever again."

"I just feel so bad when they don't make it, ya know? I know what it's like to be on the verge of losing someone close to you. And when I'm the one that has to deliver the bad news...," Luke's voice trailed off as he recalled how he had delivered bad news three times that day.

"Luke, we will have a lot of time to talk about this. Trust me; this definitely won't be the only time. I have not put you in this profession to be constantly tormented by the thought of death. I don't want it to hurt you like this."

"I'm not the one hurting though. It's just hard for me to see others hurting and dying every day, that's all."

"So typical of you to diagnose yourself, Dr. Oz." Luke smiled. "But you *are* hurting, Luke. You may not think you are, but I know you are. And this is where you need more of me. I want your view of life to change."

Luke was puzzled. His physician continued. "Do you remember when you used to have that special meet up place with your friends when you were a kid? You all used to call it 'the spot'?"

Luke pictured the place in his mind, your typical '80s baby treehouse birthed out of efforts to try and imitate the cool clubhouses shown in movies. What in reality looked like the oversized nest of a deranged bird, to Luke and his friends, it was a castle. They had to repair their clubhouse on an almost daily basis but were proud to have something that required their care. Luke was always the one who had to leave early because he had to be home by six o'clock instead of seven like his other friends, which was somewhat embarrassing at the time. But knowing he'd see everyone at the spot the next day gave him so much to look forward to that it didn't bother him that much.

Luke smiled at the memory. *Oh, to be a kid again, where my only concern was meeting up at the spot.*

His physician continued to paint the picture in Luke's mind, building off the fond memories that had entered into his thoughts. "Well, envision you and me there at the spot. We'd spend a lot of time there; it was our favorite place. But then one day you had to leave the spot for a little while, kind of like how you used to go home earlier than your friends did. So you left, but I stayed. The plan was for you to leave and then meet me back at the spot later. That is more or less how your life is, Luke. You and I were at the spot in the beginning, and then when it was time for you to be born, you left the spot, came here, and lived your life. So when it's time for you to return, you'll come back to the spot, and I'll be right there waiting for you."

"I see," Luke said slowly. The picture that had been painted in his mind became much clearer. Who knew that such a simple analogy could mean so much? "I'll meet back up with you at the spot."

"Yes, you will. One day you'll come right back to where you started. And now it's time for Samiyah to meet me at the spot, and I'll be there waiting. And this is why you really need to pray for her son." His tone grew serious again. "He doesn't have much time left, and he doesn't believe in me."

Whoa, that is a dangerous combination, Luke thought.

Now that he had more of an understanding, Luke knew that in time this would get easier to deal with, but right now it was all a bit difficult for him to take in.

Do I just drop everything and minister to her son? What do I do about Samiyah? When do I pray for her son and how do I—

"Luke, take it easy. It's going to be okay. Continue being the best doctor you can be. Be present with the family, take good care of Samiyah, and pray—*pray*—for her son. Even though he's sad right now, his sadness pales in comparison to where he'll end up if he continues to reject me. That's really why your job is so important. Remember, for everyone you encounter, I know what their bodies and their souls need. When you don't seek me first, you'll just focus on what *you* think their bodies need. Your profession requires that you focus on the physical, but your calling requires you to focus on the spiritual as well.

Because if their body is healed but their soul is dead, they will not be better off. Not at all."

Luke sat in quiet contemplation of everything he had just received: the spot, Samiyah, her son. By the time Luke's pager went off moments later, he was finally at peace. He still had some questions, but his prayer had given him what he needed to get through the rest his shift. He knew that he would be continually learning how to process everything he had just received. Plus there would always be time to follow up with his physician, even in the midst of chaos.

"Thank you for always being on call," Luke said before leaving the break room.

Nauseous Nostalgia

*I*t almost looked like a typical college party scene: bonds of friendship being forged amongst strangers in the bathroom, the bored restroom attendant selling hook-up geared toiletries, an occasional mascara-smeared face exiting a stall with her head down. And here we have these two ladies, one on the verge of throwing up in her mouth, the other trying to help her to not throw up in her mouth.

"Girl, just *breathe*! You gotta slow down and catch your breath."

Fairly certain that if it had been that simple, Nauseated Nancy would've already done that. But that was not the case. What triggered her nausea in the first place was quite extraordinary.

"I just, I just can't be-*lieve* I used to do that!" Tanna said as soon as she was somewhat able to catch her breath. "Just the thought of it makes me—"

Another heave wracked her body.

"What are you talking about?" Her friend Alma was now thoroughly confused. "What made you sick like this, out of nowhere? What's going on?"

"Please ... just gimme a minute." Tanna pressed her back against the wall and closed her eyes. The past few moments leading up to this had been a blur, so pausing to collect her thoughts seemed the best way forward.

It had all started with a Facebook memory. *Darn those Facebook memories and all the subsequent feels!*

About twelve years ago Tanna had drunkenly thought it would be a good idea to post a profile picture of herself scantily clad, in the back of a car being driven by someone who was also drunk, heading to the club. The picture alone snitched that she was as high as a kite; there was no denying it. The wry smile on her face indicated that all was well with her soul in that moment, despite the copious amounts of alcohol pumping through her 130-pound frame.

Vulnerable.

Weak.

Party girl.

Clubhead.

Fast.

All these words pulsed through her head twelve years later as she looked at herself in the picture. She was looking at a lost soul, someone who would be labeled, someone dressed for the purpose of attracting the wrong kind of attention. She was young with big dreams, but she had placed herself in harm's way and seemingly refused to look back. She put those dreams on pause night after night and justified it because *Hey, girls just wanna have fun.*

Tanna remembered those times. Pre-gaming before heading out so that they wouldn't have to buy drinks at the club, refusing to go out and party unless and until she was either drunk or high, scanning the club for potential suitors, eating like a wild bear after a night of partying, waking up the next day and laughing at the drunken pictures, texts, stories, and memories with her friends, eager to do it all over again.

Good God. That had been her life. Looking forward to getting drunk and partying. Making sure she exposed as much skin as possible without being *too* trashy. Getting frustrated if no one wanted to go out or go as hard as her if they did go out. A complete mess in which she used to be completely happy.

"Oh, God," was all she could manage to say when she looked into the eyes lazily staring back at her from the picture. "This is who I used to be."

Tanna couldn't delete that picture fast enough, though deep down, she was somewhat grateful for the memory. Later on she would realize even more that she needed to see this. She needed to see how far she had come, and she needed to be grateful that she had made it out alive. There were so many instances where she had been drunk behind the wheel, been driven by someone who was drunk, been pulled over while being underage and drunk, and countless other nights where the angels assigned to her had to pull an all-nighter. At any point she could've easily lost her life, having risked it time and time again.

It's not that Tanna didn't care about her life back then; she had just been so consumed with the wrong things that she ran out of time to care about any potential harm. Because who had time to sit and worry about the future? Life was a party.

Now Tanna was beginning to feel dizzy. She just had to get away, and the urge to run was too strong. She darted out of the pizza parlor without saying a word and ran to the next closest building. Unfortunately, the pizza spot was in a pretty sketchy area—as the best pizza spots usually are—so the next closest building ended up being a hole-in-the-wall club, which made her dizziness even worse. A few feet in from the doorway, she stopped, and the world seemed to spin around her. It was loud. The smell of smoke and alcohol was overwhelming. Everywhere she turned, there were hordes of people making horrible decisions: people slumped over the bar with drinks in hand, guys trying way too hard, and lines of people waiting to get in so they could make bad decisions too. Behind her, she could hear Alma calling her name, which snapped her out of her daze. In a panic she darted toward the bathroom so that at the very least she wouldn't throw up in public.

In the bathroom her mind was still a flurry, and her dear Alma was utterly confused. Thinking of how she got into the bathroom caused her to open her eyes and gain her footing. Her thoughts consoled her.

Okay, okay. Everything is okay.

"Sorry about that; I'm gonna be okay," she assured Alma and herself. "I just had a moment."

As she thought about her current surroundings, the irony that she ended up in a club of all places was laughable.

What next? Am I gonna fall into a black hole full of my ex-boyfriends? Goodness! And to think, this all started with me looking at a picture of myself.

Why and how this moment happened completely caught her off guard, but as her heartbeat slowed and her breathing returned to normal, she felt thankful.

God sure had to reach waaay down to save me.

Walking back to her car, with Alma's arm around her shoulders, the world became alright again.

I made it. I really made it out. Not that my life was some horror show, but the very fact that I'm alive and well right now? My God!

"You know, we never really stop to think about what could've happened," Tanna said. "We look back on our crazy college days now and then, but we don't think about the fact that we actually made it out. How many people have we heard about that got killed in car accidents, ended up in jail, got murdered—all while doing the exact same things we used to do every night? And don't even get me started on the guys that we barely knew, how we would be quick to hop in their cars or go to their houses. Anything could have happened to us! But we never think about that part. We just kinda moved on from it and grew up. But it's true; we got saved every single time we went out without even realizing it. Night after night our lives got saved from dangers that we kept putting ourselves in. It's unbelievable. To get saved once is awesome by itself, but to keep getting saved? I just … I can't even believe it."

Some young girls whizzed by them on the sidewalk with excited chatter.

"Oh my God, girl!" one laughed to her friend.

The entire group laughed and swayed drunkenly down the sidewalk, heading toward the club where bad decisions were made.

Snickering at the group, Alma said, "Yeah, we used to be just like those lil' fast girls. Kids these days, uh uh uh."

"Wait now, Alma; they're not fast. They may be lost, just like we were. Confused. Trying to find their way. We gotta stop judging, sis. We were doing the same thing as them not that long ago, and woulda threw hands if someone called us fast. You know I'm right!" They both smiled in agreement. "And besides, we were fortunate enough to make it out of that lifestyle, so let's pray that they make it out too."

Lord, keep them.

We refuse to judge them because we used to be them.

We rebuke car accidents, abuse, violence,

Everything you saved us from when we were in the world,

Lord, save those girls from those things too.

Encamp angels around them tonight, oh Lord.

If they don't have a personal relationship with you,

God, I ask that you put them on the path for that to happen as soon as possible, in the Name of Jesus.

We pray with our whole hearts that they live long enough to look back, and thank you for bringing them out too. In Jesus' name, amen.

꩜

Not to Remember

I couldn't remember the last time I had seen Grandma. After quarantine took over, grandparents all over the world were officially off-limits. It was such a scary realization for me, considering that our elderly loved ones wouldn't always be here with us, and this pandemic further restricted the amount of time we had left to spend with them.

Now more than ever, I really needed her hug and sweet words. She was always so excited to see me. Lately, I had been feeling super invisible, like I was only needed when someone wanted something from me. I felt like no one was really excited to see me and that I just kind of existed. But Grandma, she knew how to make me feel like a million bucks.

I couldn't get to her fast enough. I had been playing out our reunion in my head for months. We would hug for at least an hour, take some selfies, I would make her some coffee and fix her something to eat, she would eventually ask me about my wedding plans, and I would have to remind her that I was still super single. I couldn't wait. It would be so good to see her.

"Hi, Grandma, I missed you!"

I gave her a warm hug. Her short frame always made me feel at home. I inhaled deeply, sucking the life out of every second of our embrace.

"Oh, hi darling," she said sweetly. I could feel a soft pat on my back. "You're so kind." She awkwardly pulled away from me after a few seconds and took a step back. Speaking to the caretaker standing next to me, she explained, "She used to be one of my students. Isn't she sweet?"

My heart melted. Even fully aware that she didn't remember me anymore, her words still stung. They would continue to hang in the air over me for a long time. How could something make someone you love forget you ever existed? I pulled her close again, knowing that I was probably doing so in vain. Still, I hoped deep in my soul that she would remember me again.

***

That night I poured my heart out to God about how I was feeling. It was the only thing I could do to process the emotions stemming from the day. My heart was hurting.

Then, something beautiful happened.

God showed me that He understood exactly how I was feeling. The same way I had felt about Grandma not remembering me was similar to how God felt when His children do not remember Him. My story was His story too. In His own words, God described how my experience today was much like the experiences He had with some of His loved ones:

"Hi, beloved!"

It was so good seeing her. I missed her a lot.

"I missed you!" I gave her a warm hug. Her short frame always made me feel at home. I inhaled deeply, sucking the life out of every second of our embrace.

"Oh, hi there," she said sweetly. I could feel a soft pat on my back. "You're so kind." She awkwardly pulled away from me and took a step back. Speaking to her friend standing next to me, she explained, "This used to be my friend back in the day. Isn't he sweet?"

My heart melted. Even fully aware that she didn't believe in me anymore, her words still stung. They would continue to hang in the air over me for a long time. How could something make someone you love deny that you ever existed? I pulled her close again, knowing that I was probably doing so in vain. Still, I hoped deep in my soul that she would believe in me again.

God's relatable story put my mind at ease. My situation had not changed—the hurt was definitely still there—but knowing that He understood and experienced what I was going through truly touched me. I had often been frustrated when I would tell someone something and they would automatically respond with *I understand* even though there was no way they could truly understand since they had not been in my shoes. But God's *I understand* hit different because I knew He was telling the truth.

Even though this pain was something I had to go through, I was thankful that the God Who Understands would walk me through it.

Stroll Down Memory's Train

*In the year that King Uzziah died, I saw the Lord
sitting on a throne, high and lifted up, and the train of
His robe filled the temple.*

Isaiah 6:1

"Wait, wait, wait," Niecy pleaded as her laughter subsided. "You mean to tell me that you physically kicked him out? Like, with your actual feet?"

"You know I get a *kick* out of being the boss!"

The fact that his pun was intended sent them both over the edge. Their wild laughter filled the universe around them.

"So what did he say right before you let him have it?" Niecy tried to picture the scene in her head. "I can't even imagine what he was thinking."

"Ahh, he was all like: *Don't. Push. Me. Cuz, I'm. Close. To. The. Edge.*"

Dad singing the famous rap verse took them completely out again. Light years passed before they were able to stop laughing again.

"And that, my friend, is why he's such a hater." Dad sat back in his overly plush seat as a satisfied grin spread across his face.

Niecy resumed her stroll down memory's train, her eyes landing on another piece of velvety fabric attached to her father's robe. She picked it up and read the writing on it. "And this, remember this?!" Niecy held it up to his face. "I heard this was *epic*!"

"Of course, how could I forget? The whole world knows about that one."

They roared with laughter for the millionth time. It was the kind of laughter that made you laugh harder because you laughed at how your laugh sounded. Every attempt to regain composure failed miserably, but it was well with their souls. The melodies of their shrieks and giggles, peppered with gasps for air, danced and echoed into eternity.

"Oh, now here's one I used to read about all the time." Niecy read the script on the fabric out loud, as this piece was one of many that were spread across the temple floor. From start to finish, it would take one thousand lifetimes to go through all of them; there were just that many. But Niecy had plenty of time to spare and so did Dad. To top it off, they were spending this time together, something Niecy had longed to do ever since she could remember.

"Number 1,364,572. The soldiers made their beds at the bottom of the sea. Hashtag: *Red Sea. Hashtag: swimmin' with the fishes.* Ouch!" she exclaimed in mock horror. "Cold world!"

"Yep. Talk about dearly de-*part*-ed."

Another round of laughter, their cackles loud enough to make the angels in Heaven wonder what the *heck* was so funny.

Another piece of the never-ending train of fabric caught Niecy's eye. "Number 773,521: Looked death in the face, said: *You lose* and dropped the mic." Niecy beamed. "Mic drop? Dad, really?"

"Had to." He grinned and popped his proverbial collar to signify swag. It worked.

"Dad, you're the best!" Niecy ran to him and jumped into his arms. He was her world, and she was his.

"I love you so much, baby girl. Now, I want you to find number 2,316,444. It's down the hall by the doorposts. I have something to tell you."

Niecy gave Dad a tight squeeze and then leaped into her mission. After quite some time, she found the fabric bearing the number and held it in her hands.

"Got it!"

Her excitement quieted as she read the fabric, and her countenance began to change with each word. When she finished reading, she could feel everything around her standing still. She read it again. And a third time. She glanced at Dad, whose face was full of compassion. He leaned forward in his seat. His love for Niecy was palatable, pricking the depths of her heart.

She read aloud. "I changed her mother's mind so that my child could live."

A parade of images poured from Niecy's heart and flashed through her mind: her fifteen year-old mother, pregnant and nauseous, running out of the clinic; the delivery room on her birthdate, full of confusion and loneliness; her mother holding her for the very first time, a child with a smaller child.

Niecy closed her eyes. "I never thanked you for that, for changing my mom's mind. Dad, thank you for giving me a chance."

"Oh, but you did, in your own special way." He walked toward her, the thick train of his robe dragging behind him in a dramatic display. "When you and I would talk, I knew that in your heart you were just happy to be alive. No matter how bad things got, you were always glad to live just one more day."

"It doesn't hurt like it used to," Niecy confessed. "In fact, it doesn't hurt at all. But I know that when I was down there, I always felt like a huge mistake. Like I didn't have a place to belong. The way people treated me just made me …,"

They embraced. Before, she had a diminished mental capacity and was unable to walk, and she often heard celebrities, doctors, and even presidential candidates support aborting children that would be born with the same conditions she had. According to what she had heard, many people felt it was better if children like her were aborted since she would be disabled, born into poverty, and a financial burden to her teenage mother. Knowing that the most powerful people in the world had this mindset was extremely depressing to Niecy. Because of that, she grew up feeling as though she was marked and that no one wanted her around simply because of who she was.

"I know, my love. The world is a cruel place indeed. But Niecy, I have always wanted to be your father. From the beginning of time, I planned to be your father. Your life showed so many people my love." He walked to the other doorpost, looked to the floor, and immediately found what he was looking for. "Here it is. Number 9,500,212: I brought Niecy back to her real home." He spun around in a circle, arms extended. "So, how do you like it?"

"I absolutely love this place, Daddy!"

They embraced again and as if on cue began to dance together. Niecy had never danced before, but she had always wanted to. For the twelve years of her life below, she imagined what her first dance would be like if she were ever able to walk. What she used to daydream about paled in comparison to what was taking place now.

They twirled to the chant of celestial songbirds, whose melodies grew louder and louder; angelic background music for the ultimate father-daughter dance. The father showing his daughter that she had always been a part of his plan, a daughter being able to see how much she was truly valued and wanted. The heavenlies worked together to create the perfect atmosphere for the father and his beloved child. Their steps sent bolts of lightning through the clouds and into the world below. Thunder boomed with each spin and twirl.

"Welcome to forever, baby girl."

Niecy's dream of dancing had finally come true. And now that she was home, she would never have to dance alone.

***

After her first dance Niecy began to write from the place of inspiration and understanding that she now had. She wanted others to be inspired and encouraged while they lived and before they came home to Dad. She penned her writing in a way that would touch the hearts of those who had lives like hers, so that they would know that Dad had planned to be their father too. She wanted to encourage them that one day, their dance with Dad would make all things new.

Before sending it off, Niecy read her letter one last time:

Psalm 139:13-16: "For You formed my inward parts; You covered me in my mother's womb. I will praise You, for I am fearfully and wonderfully made; Marvelous are Your works, And that my soul knows very well. My frame was not hidden from You, When I was made in secret, And skillfully wrought in the lowest parts of the earth. Your eyes saw my substance, being yet unformed. And in Your book they all were written, The days fashioned for me, When as yet there were none of them."

Dear Family,

At first glance, this psalm makes it quite obvious that none of us are here by mistake. We were all planned by God. Regardless of how you were brought into this world, God planned to be your parent.

Psalm 139 has been called King David's song of support. When he wrote it he had a lot going on in his life. His family didn't really see his value, his mentor Saul turned into his worst enemy, his wife Michal was embarrassed by him, and his own son Absalom tried to kill him. King David went through *a lot*. So it's no surprise that some of his psalms reveal how he encouraged himself when times were tough. In Psalm 139, he spends time acknowledging God's hand on his life before he was even born. Why do you think he took the time to point this out?

Verse 13 says that God formed the *inward parts*, which are our essential organs. Modern technology has shown that our inward parts are the first things that are formed just a few weeks after conception. Piece by piece. One day at a time. God, in His infinite wisdom, began working on the part of us that was necessary for our survival, the inward parts. We know that if our inward parts completely stop working, then we would die. But the reverse is not true. Because even if our outward parts don't work, our inward parts can still function. For example, a person with no legs can still live, but a person with no heart or no brain could not. It's our inward parts that make the difference, and perhaps that's why God started there first.

Those with physical and mental disabilities still have functioning blood vessels, nervous systems, brain waves, all these amazing parts that are working inwardly around the clock. They have a ton of activity going on in their inward parts, and God orchestrates all that activity on a daily basis. Their inward parts can function just as good as someone with no physical or mental disability. So we're all the same when it comes to the inside, which is the most important part. But too often we focus on a person's outward parts and judge them. God is not just a god of outward appearance; He is God of the inward parts, the parts that make the difference.

In verse 13 we also see that God knit us together while we were in our mother's womb. The word knit is *cakak* in Hebrew, and it means to cover; protect; a defense; to fence in. Part of God's process in forming us required Him to cover us. I repeat: part of God's process in forming us required Him to cover us. God's covering is not just one of the things He does for us, it is literally part of how He made us. He had to cover us in order to form us.

My friend, you have been covered for a very long time, since the dawn of creation. He formed you while you were in your mother's womb. Once you were born, He kept waiting for you to grow, go through life, and finally receive Him. When you think about it, that is a very long time to wait. From the dawn of creation until now; through all that time, God planned to be your parent.

Verse 15 declares that we were *intricately woven in the depths of the earth.* When you weave something it takes time, precision, a keen attention to detail, and patience. If you've ever seen your grandmother weaving a blanket, chances are that you never sat and watched her weave it from start to finish. You may have seen her start on it, put it down, come back to it the next day, and so on. That's because it is very rare for someone to sit down and weave an entire blanket in one day. They often work on it piece by piece, one day at a time. That is why handmade items are much more expensive than those made by a machine. The level of detail that goes into something that is handmade is much more valuable than any man-ufactured product. The texture is better, the de-tails are more vibrant, and it just feels a bit better knowing that what you have was handmade.

The text makes a point to clarify that we weren't just woven but we were *intricately* woven. The Hebrew word for this is *raqam*, and it means to mix colors; to weave with variously colored threads. Using different colors takes an addition-al amount of time in the weaving process because you literally have to stitch with one color, stop, pick another color, stitch, stop, pick another col-or, and so on. When weaving with one color, you can stitch without having to stop. But if you want it intricately woven, then it is going to require much more of your time.

Isn't it amazing that the most detailed, time-consuming method is what describes God's process in creating us? It wouldn't make a bit of sense for God to spend all this time and detail on something just to call it a mistake. That would be like someone "mistakenly" building a huge sky-scraper and then looking at it and saying: *Oops, I didn't mean to build that skyscraper; that was a mistake.* Sounds weird, right? Well that's how we sound when we try to convince ourselves that we were born by mistake. We are not mistakes; we are intricately woven!

Knowing that you were intricately woven, can't you see that God didn't simply throw you togeth-er? You were not mass-produced like a doll in a factory. God didn't do you like He did the light, and the waters, and the land, which He simply spoke into existence. He could've easily just said a word and *boom*! you could have appeared. No. Instead God took His careful time and intricately wove you together.

Another important point is that God's planned parenthood is not just limited to those of us who lived long enough to be birthed into this world. Verse 16 shows that God saw our *unformed substance* when what we are made of had not even formed yet. He saw us before He began weaving us together. God's love and covering are not predicated on whether a person is actually birthed into this world or not. Nothing in Scripture says that. Whether we only lived for one trimester or were born and lived to be one hundred years old, we were all an unformed substance at one point, and that is when God saw us. God spends time with *all* of his children because all of us were planned by Him.

So now do you see why King David acknowledged God's hand on his life before he was even born? Knowing that you were planned by the Creator of the universe, formed with inward parts, purposely covered, and intricately woven should definitely encourage you.

My friends, do not worry about what other people see when they look at you. Start seeing yourself as God sees you: His beloved, priceless work of art.

Anyone can take a picture. Anyone can write down some words. But only an artist can create a real masterpiece. God is the Master Artist, and He absolutely, 100 percent, planned to be your parent.

The Most Special Delivery

Grabbing her mother's ankles, which were covered in a soft, white sheet, she began to pull. Her arm and shoulder muscles stretched tightly beneath her skin as she pulled her mother's body toward her.

"Two down, two more to go," she said, attempting to add more motivation to the arduous task. It didn't work.

Slowly she took one step backward, then another, her mother's body dragging along as she pulled. After a few steps she paused, her chest heaving with each breath. She placed her hands on her knees, waiting for her breathing to return to normal. The sun blazed hotly on her skin. Her back was beginning to ache, and overall she was just plain tired.

"Good Lord, I'm really doing this."

Her two children had been super easy to move; they were both very light. But what really made them so easy to move was that she truly had no other option. She hadn't been able to see them in months, she lived on the other side of the world, and it was only by some miracle that she had been able to stay in contact with them after everything that had happened. Her children were still young, so they had their whole lives ahead of them. Doing this was the best thing she could have possibly done for them.

Grabbing her mother's ankles again, she pressed her own feet firmly into the ground for support. She had quickly learned that starting off with one big pull helped to set the tone for the rest of the trek. She closed her eyes and pulled. Nothing happened. Her mother's body was being a bit stubborn this time. Typical.

"Come *on*."

She pulled again, barely moving anything. She knew there was no obstruction causing this; the path forward was clear and smooth.

It must be me again.

Not wanting to waste any more of her effort, she stood up and examined her mother's linen-covered form. She closed her eyes again and tried to focus.

Pushing the negative voices out of her head, she envisioned herself letting go of her mother. She pictured a strong sense of relief washing over her as she bid farewell to the mother she loved dearly. *It's time for me to let you go* she saw herself saying. Her mother's face faded away into the background, with a look that was hard to read.

Opening her eyes again she began to pray. "God, please help me do this. I know I need to. It's hard enough for me to let go, but I feel like Ma doesn't want me to let her go. She needs me."

The tears began to flow despite her attempts to hold them in. Up until now the day had been full of fighting, crying, and torment. She was physically drained. The mental exhaustion had crept in hours ago.

"Lord, please give me strength. I know this is Your will, but it's just so hard. I love her, and it feels like I'm just throwing her away. She doesn't want me to let her go, but I have to. I'm not even asking You to change this. I just—please, just help me."

Help was all she could think to ask for in the moment. Her prayer had been sincere. She had finally gotten the courage to accept what needed to be done, but then she realized that it was her mother's desire to stay that was really pulling at her heart. They had always been close. They had supported each other through a nasty divorce, they had raised a child together, they had buried their beloved son/brother, and many more difficult situations over the span of thirty-three years. They talked every day, mostly laughing, complaining, and humorously over-exaggerating simple experiences. They felt like home to one another, wherever they were. But now, God Himself wanted their relationship to shift, and she felt as though she had been asked to carve out her heart with her own hands and leave it behind. Her mother had been her world.

"God, it would be *so* much easier if You would just come down and do this Yourself. I think I can let her go. But knowing that she doesn't want to *be* let go hurts the most." She had been required to do so much that it felt like she was entirely overwhelmed. The weight of the world seemed to be resting directly on her shoulders, and it was beyond painful.

Eventually, her confession gave her the second wind she needed—literally and figuratively. There was no other explanation for the source of the strength she now had to continue. In those moments her mindset shifted from *I can't do this because my mother doesn't want me to let go* to *I can do this,* even if *my mother doesn't want me to let go.* The *even if* part made all the difference.

She bent down to grab her mother's ankles again. "I love you, Ma."

She pulled through her exhaustion, past the evil whispers in her head, and past the memories she had shared with her mother. She pulled through, forcing herself to keep going. She pulled so hard that she almost fell backward into the place where her children were. Regaining her balance, she slid her mother next to the spot where her son was, smoothing out the edges of the linen sheet. As she did this her mother's hand dropped out from under the sheet. She beheld the scene for a moment, accepting the piercing irony of it all.

"I can't, Ma. I have to let you go." She tenderly kissed her mother's hand and placed it back under the sheet.

Jesus ...

Standing back up, she looked out toward her father's form in the distance. She was now standing in the space where she needed to bring him, but her feet were glued to the floor. The thought of even walking toward her father sent waves of panic through her veins.

Lord, how am I going to do this?

She knew that the obvious answer was that she would let go of her father the same way she had found the strength to let go of her mother and children. Yet the thought of going through this a fourth time overwhelmed her. By this point she felt as though she had already placed her entire life into one empty place, and she had nothing left to give. Her heart cried, *Daddy too?* It was unfathomable that one person could be required to give up so much.

You're right; it is unfair. You shouldn't have to do anything else; you've already done enough. Just stop. You don't have to do this.

These thoughts flooded her mind again, as they had so many times before. The same whispers, same emotions, same desire to give in and give up. This time the resistance was much harder to come by. She really wanted to give up. She felt as though she deserved—and had worked hard enough—to agree that her work was finished.

She was now standing over her father, whose large body was wrapped in the familiar white sheet. Fortunately the negative voices in her head did not cause her to stop moving; instead, they propelled her forward. She recited Philippians 4:13 over and over to physically drown out those voices, repeating each word as loud as she could. Her determination not to give in, as she had done repeatedly in the past, had now won the fight against what she knew was the wrong decision.

Yes, this one is different, but if I can hand over three, then I can hand over four.

With a passion similar to rage, she grabbed her father's ankles and began to pull. She unconsciously screamed with each pull, exposing all her teeth, and biting down hard. Her legs slid forward beneath her, taking on the weight of her father's body. She fell to the ground as she pulled, at one point sliding herself backward on the ground to give herself more traction. The ferocity with which she attacked this task surprised her.

If that's what it takes to get this done, then so be it!

The ordeal was almost brutal, somewhat like a physical fight: the pain of having to do the one thing she never wanted to do, the physical task of pulling her father, and the complete sense of sorrow that kept tears constantly pooled in her eyes before they splashed down her face. Her screams tore at her own heart. She had never been like this before. She pulled her father, she dragged him, she held his legs tightly.

"I love you, Daddy! I love you so much!" she said in between pulls. She finally collapsed onto his chest and lay there crying. "I really, really love you."

She sat up and examined what must have been the most pitiful scene in the world: a mourning daughter crying over her father, sweating, bruised, and exhausted. "Daddy, you're the hardest one to let go."

Her father had lost his mother when he was a child, he struggled with several chronic illnesses, and he had the unwanted task of burying his only son a few years ago. Her heart grieved for her father, at times because of the physical pain he had experienced, and at other times because of the mental anguish he went through. She had done her best to help her father and bring him out of depression, but it was overwhelming. There was just so much.

Her father was stubborn, and he often resisted help from others because their advice involved healthier eating habits, more exercise, and all the *blah blah blah* that he never wanted to hear. The emotions she went through regarding her father ranged from resentment for not taking better care of his health, to compassion over the loss of his childhood, to the undeniable joy that fathers and daughters share. It was a lot. And now in this place, she felt that all the fighting, begging, uplifting, loving she had done over the years was going down the drain because it left them here, with her crying over him.

The passion she had before was now nowhere to be seen. She was completely and utterly broken. With not even a sign of life left in her, she was somehow able to stand up again. Her expression was empty. Her clothes were torn and filthy, her dreads spun outwards in a million different directions, and she had no will to bother wiping away her sweat or her tears. Her nose began to run, so she breathed out of her mouth. She robotically continued pulling her father. She wasn't making as much progress as she had before, but she eventually reached the place that held the rest of her family.

Her mind had completely checked out, and she was now operating in the same manner as a machine. She pulled her father into a space next to her mother. She didn't bother adjusting his linen sheet as she had done with the others. In her fight to move him, the sheet had fallen away from his legs and lower torso, leaving his upper body and face covered.

After standing there for a while, she slumped in between her father and her mother and stayed there, looking at her father. The tears continued to flow, but her eyes were still blank. She was in a daze. Although she had technically succeeded in her task of bringing her family here, somewhere along the way, the task had depleted her emotions. She wasn't relieved, she wasn't emotional, she just ... was. A part of her couldn't believe that she had done it, and the other part of her didn't want to believe that she had done it. These two parts weighed heavily in her heart. She lay her head on her father's chest and closed her eyes.

Nothing came to her. No words, no eloquent goodbyes— nothing. She just lay there because she didn't know what else to do. When she was finally able to sit up, her family was still there, still lying side-by-side, still covered and motionless. She stood up and stepped back to take all four of them into view.

"I love you, but I'm not going to say goodbye. And I can't come back." After one more look, she turned and walked away.

***

Later that evening she contemplated everything that had happened earlier.

I doubt anyone will ever understand what I did, but that's okay. I had to do it.

The unfamiliar, almost eerie feeling of letting go of your family with no assurance of what would happen next was constantly in the back of her mind. She had handed them all over with no guarantees. How could someone do that to their family? She often asked this question when she saw news stories of murder-suicides and the like, lamenting over the loss of life in general, but the loss of family on a deeper level. In her mind the act of leaving your own family was one of the gravest offenses imaginable.

Her ringing phone snatched her out of her morbid reverie. It was her mother.

Oh shoot, I'm late for dinner.

"Hey, Ma."

"Where are you?"

No *Hello*, no *How are you*, no greeting whatsoever. Typical mom behavior. They do all the things you would get yelled at for doing. Gotta love it.

"I got held up, Ma. I'm gonna get ready and then head over in a bit."

She mentally prepared what she would wear, knowing that she would definitely wear glasses tonight to conceal her puffy eyes.

"I coulda swore I told you to be here at seven."

"Maaaa, I'm coming. I'll be there soon."

"Well, hurry it up; we hungry!" she said before saying goodbye and hanging up.

She headed straight for the shower and vigorously washed her face and body. She was really looking forward to seeing her mom and children. The kids would be returning to school soon, and she looked forward to taking them shopping for new clothes. After spending a few days with them, she would make the three-hour drive to see her father and check in with his doctors. She couldn't wait.

After putting on lotion, she walked over to her closet and mechanically snatched down the clothes she had previously planned to wear. She threw them onto her bed before going to fetch her iron. When she returned to her room, the white sheets on her bed caught her attention, causing her to freeze. The vivid flashback of what she had done with her family took her by surprise.

She had surrendered her family, one by one, leaving them in the hands of the One she trusted the most. It had taken years for her to get to this point, but she had finally done it. God had required her to trust them to Him, instead of her trying to save them all by herself. Trying to save her family had nearly killed her. She spent years convinced that she had loved them too much to ever let them go, especially considering all that they had been through. But she finally gave them all to God, not fully knowing what was on the other side of that surrender.

Her family had been the one thing that she had refused to let go of after her brother's passing. She figured that if she held onto them and made sure they had what they needed, then they would be alright. Plus, she felt that God would understand her decision to take care of them and would allow her to tightly cling to them since she no longer had her brother to cling to. But she had been wrong. Very wrong.

In no uncertain terms God had shown her that caring for her family was His job. Her father, mother, and children belonged to Him first. And the truth was she hadn't trusted anyone with them, not even God. So God required her to surrender her family to Him, and eventually, sorrowfully, she did. It wasn't until after she had fully surrendered them that she could trust that God knew what was best for all of them. Placing them in His hands was the best place she could leave them.

"I *really* did it. And it didn't kill me. It definitely hurt, but it didn't kill me. Thank you."

She finished getting dressed and headed for the door as her mother called her phone again.

Part III

WHAT THEY SEE:

An Angelic Perspective

Fascinated

"*I* really, *really* don't feel like dancing right now."

I was just trying to explain myself, but what I was doing wasn't talking. I was practically crying out for help.

"Trust me. You need to dance. I want you to."

That was the short answer I got. Welp, I guess I was just supposed to suck it up and be okay with that answer. Forget the fact that the male population in my family seemed to be dwindling by the moment. There had been three funerals on my dad's side in just one month. Worst. Summer. Ever. Oh, and not to mention that my heart was already broken right before this all started happening. And I just really, really wanted to sleep right now. At least when I slept, I could dream of something other than my life.

"I promise; I will dance my heart out tomorrow. I *promise*. I just need to stop. I need a break. This is too much."

I plopped myself on the floor without even trying to. Great. Not only am I crying, but my own legs decided to give up on me too. I didn't even mean to sit down just now, but I did. Lord!

"Please, please, please, please," I said, more to myself this time. My head was now tucked tightly between my knees, and I hugged my legs together for balance and support in the shaky place I found myself in. "I just need a break. I don't want to do this right now. I'm not even a dancer!"

Silence.

"I *can't* do this right now. I can't and I won't."

Minutes passed. I cried harder. The sky overhead grew darker with thick, heavy gray clouds. I was certain that because my life was basically falling apart that I did not have to do anything I didn't want to do. I had been through enough. What was a dance going to do for me anyway?

"This dance isn't for you. It's for me."

Another short and not-so-sweet answer. I wanted to scream, so I did.

But I'm the one going through. I'm the one that needs to be comforted. No disrespect, but can someone come and do something for me *right now? I am running on empty!*

These thoughts and questions ran circles around my mind. The song I was supposed to be dancing to continued to play. It was a beautiful melody titled *Angels*.

Over and over it played.

"Sure wish I could see one right now."

I burst into tears again, this time, simply because I felt so alone. I'd heard of people having angelic visitations all the time, but I had never really experienced one before. This song was a bittersweet reminder of that fact.

"Now would be a perfect time, God. A perfect time."

The song continued. It really was quite beautiful. The singer, Khalid, had a relaxed, calming voice, and I loved to hear him sing. Even when he just repeated the word *angels* over and over, it was still magical. Because sometimes, repetition is good.

He sang about seeing angels in his living room, describing their fragrance and the places that they walked and slept. Wow. It must be nice to see angels so much that you could pen a song about seeing them. Khalid was winning.

Great.

I'm out here, crying on the floor, storms brewing outside, and I'm low-key jealous that I don't get to see angels like Khalid does. What is my life right now?

"You're fascinated by angels?" The question threw me off.

"Well, yeah." I wiped my face with the back of my hand. "I'm fascinated by angels, and I wish I could see one right now," I added, somewhat hopefully, somewhat sharply.

"Well, I'm fascinated by you."

I didn't know what to say. I remembered the fascination, the images, and the thoughts that I'd had about angels my entire life. Quiet regularly I would stop and picture myself being in awe of an angelic presence. I imagined how my heart would race, how I would be overwhelmed that something I had always hoped to see was finally happening. I tried to think of what I would say, what I would do in that moment. I mean, what's the protocol for an angelic visitation? My guess was that there was no protocol. It just happened, and you simply let it happen.

If I ever saw an angel, I'm sure I would just stand still in awe, unable to move. I would do my best to focus on every little detail, capturing each second in my mind so that it would stay with me forever. I would try to speak, but even if I couldn't, I would be content with just finally being in the presence of an angel. And once the angel left, I would probably beg for it to come back, and maybe even run after it. How awesome would it be to speak from experience about a visitation and no longer have to imagine what it would be like?

Yeah, that would be pretty amazing.

I was thankful for the detour in my thoughts. It felt much better than crying. And then I remembered the words of the One Who Speaks to Me:

"Well, I'm fascinated by you."

With even more fascination than I had about angels, I realized, He was fascinated by me. Everything I did captivated Him. Every time I came into His presence, His heart beat faster. When I danced for Him, when I worshipped Him, it changed something in His world. He stopped whatever He was doing and just let the moment with me happen. He let Himself get the fullness of everything I did, so that He could remember it forever. He refused to take His eyes off of me, and He didn't dare let anything break His concentration. Because He was fascinated with me.

And then it all made sense. He desired to see me, to have me do things for Him. The way I desired, even begged, to encounter an angel, to have that experience for myself, was the same way He desired to watch me, to be with me. I was an amazing experience for Him.

I could taste the familiar verses in my mouth. Very sweet. Psalm 8:4-5 easily poured from my heart and flowed out of me:

What is man that You are mindful of him,

And the son of man that You visit him?

For You have made him a little lower than the angels,

And You have crowned him with glory and honor.

Because my heart was already so open, my tear ducts soon got the memo and cranked back into overdrive. This time my tears were for the weight of this revelation. If the One Who Speaks to Me wants me to do something, why don't I just do it? Why do I always have to make everything about me and what I'm going through? Why does He even deal with someone like me?

Goodness. I don't deserve Him. I never did.

"My love, I've crowned you with glory and honor," He repeated the verse back to me, and it hit me hard. But in a good way. In the best way someone could be hit.

Wow. Only moments with the One Who Speaks to Me, and my life had changed forever. How could I not do what He asked of me? He wanted to see me even more than I wanted to see Him, and I for one knew what it was like to spend years wanting to see something. My deceased loved ones, angels, the future children that I desired to have—every day I desired to see them. I would often sit and just think of how they looked. I pictured them in my mind and carried them in my heart. I encouraged myself that one day, I would see them all. So yes, if I'm able to be the one who God wanted to see, I wasn't going to hide from Him. I wouldn't keep holding back. I wanted Him to see me because He was fascinated by me.

Fortunately, my legs had returned to their solid state, so I lifted myself up off the floor by holding onto the couch. I almost propelled myself a bit too much and stumbled forward.

God asks me to dance and the first thing I do is trip. Tuh.

But I had a feeling He didn't mind.

I pushed the back button on my phone to restart the song, put it on repeat, and took my position in the center stage of my living room.

***

Confession time: I'm a bit camera shy. I take flight when I see or sense someone reaching for their phone or camera. I guess you could say I want to preserve my image. (Pun definitely intended, and you love it.)

I actually don't mind being seen. In fact there are tons of people who see me quite regularly. And even those who never see me can sometimes sense when I'm in the neighborhood. I have a friend, for example, and I sing over him at night while he sleeps. It's something I like to do to shift the atmosphere he's living in. It's definitely not the best environment, but when I show up, I handle business for him, so he doesn't have to worry about it when he wakes up. I guess you could say that I'm kinda like a sleep aid. I just love when he wakes up with the songs that I sang stuck in his head. He's never seen me before, but he talks to God about me, so I know he feels me.

I ended up getting into a lot of fights today, but out of nowhere, my boss called on me to do something else. It was a definite change of pace. I left the battlefield and ended up in a living room. It was a woman I've seen before. She's not much of a dancer, but tonight she stole the show. I'm talking *Dancing with the Stars* theatrics. I was shocked. She had never been this way before.

I guess it had a lot to do with what happened right before she started dancing. She was inconsolable, so instinctively I began to massage her heart. From the outside it might have seemed as though it wasn't working, but fortunately I could feel what was going on inside. She was changing. This change made me ecstatic because she had been on the verge of giving up. I've had to visit her a lot lately just to massage her heart. She was going through a lot.

I know she really wanted to see me, but all I was allowed to do was be present. One day she would understand that what I did for her was much more important than her ability to see me.

Turns out that even though I was sent to help her, she ended up blessing me. I couldn't stop staring. She had always been afraid of thunderstorms. Loud, unexpected noises stressed her out. But tonight she danced *with* the storm. Lightning flashed each time she twirled, and when her feet landed on the floor, thunder roared. She smiled as she noticed the synchronization. For the first time in her life, she wasn't phased by the storm raging around her. She came alive at the thought of no longer being afraid.

Thankfully I was able to capture most of her dance on video. I would have gotten the whole thing, but I joined in myself at one point. I just had to. I can't wait to watch it again and again. She was so beautiful in that moment. A changed woman. I hugged her close as she slept tonight, and I thanked God for the smile on her lips.

One day, hopefully soon, we will dance together in God's living room.

Workmanship

*You are committed to what you create — you take
pride in it.*

Pastor Myra L. Jackson

*T*he archangel watched God circle slowly around His
masterpiece again, making slight adjustments every
so often.

Still circling, God said, "Now, I want you to protect this
one with everything you've got. Understood?" He peered over
at the archangel, looking straight into his eyes.

"Sir, yes, Sir!"

The archangel darted to the supply room to quickly scan
the inventory. The warrior in him gravitated to the swords.
He continued searching until he found the one he wanted and
then quickly returned.

"This one right here is going to help me change the world,"
God continued, giving the archangel specific instructions as
He worked on His masterpiece. "I'm not finished just yet, but
I want you to see what I've been working on."

That was music to the archangel's ears, as the masterpiece had been completely hidden from view. With one smooth motion God unveiled His masterpiece in front of the archangel.

God smiled. The archangel gasped in awe.

Standing there as God's unveiled masterpiece was *you*.

"Absolutely beautiful, my Lord."

With that God picked up each of your hands and carefully drew deep stripes on your palms to remind you of His Son. As He drew He began to sing over you:

I'll be with you always,

to the end of the age

My love written to you

Your heart is my page.

Goodbye for now,

but it won't be for long

I will tell you the rest

when you come back home.

Once He finished, He tilted your head back and gently poured living water into your mouth. In this way, you would always be filled with a symbol of His Spirit, and you wouldn't be able to live without it. He then held you close to Him. His heartbeat penetrated your chest, causing the heart that He had placed inside of you to begin beating, slowly at first, but then stronger and stronger until it beat to the same rhythm as His.

"It is finished!" God exclaimed with joy, beaming proudly at you, His masterpiece.

He hurriedly wrote something in His book before closing it. Turning His attention to the archangel, He said, "You'll be keeping a close eye on this one for me. This one is very special. In fact, this one is worth dying for."

Meanwhile

"*I* knew it!" Carter shrieked, peering into his neighbor's window. "Nasir has been stress eating. That's why he's gaining all that weight. It has nothing to do with his new meds. He comes home and stuffs his face. What a liar!"

With this new information Carter hopped off his makeshift ladder and snuck around to the back side of Nasir's house. Once there he hoisted himself onto his elbows and wiggled his way closer to the back window. He peered in closely, his eyes focused on the laptop inside of Nasir's kitchen.

"Is that a Tinder profile? You've gotta be kidding me!" He would have shaken his head in disgust, but his position prevented him from doing so. "No wonder he hasn't been cutting his grass lately. He's been too busy lookin' for love. Ha!"

He hopped down from the window and leaned against the house. He wanted to wait until the coast was clear before sneaking around to the other side of Nasir's house. That's where the best view of the bedroom was.

Glancing over toward his own house, Carter saw a small fire brewing in his garage. Both of his cars were parked there, along with many of his tools, books, and family mementos. He brushed it off and continued waiting where he was, unbothered.

Five minutes later he began the short trek to the opposite side of Nasir's house. Peering into the bedroom while simultaneously hiding himself, he had a great view of the TV. He squinted, trying to make out what show was playing on the TV. A loud blast from behind startled him, taking his focus for a brief second. He remembered the fire that had started in his own garage and concluded that the fuel from his cars probably caused the explosion. His house would likely be consumed in flames in about ten minutes. Rolling his eyes at the nuisance of the fire, he turned back to the TV screen in Nasir's bedroom.

"Well, well, well … his old wedding video. Make up your mind, buddy. Do you want a Tinder date or your ex? Are you moving on or going back? Cuz you've been crying about it for months!"

Carter laughed and with a satisfied grin, dug in his pocket for his phone. He couldn't wait to talk to his friends about what he had just seen.

"They're not gonna believe this foolishness. Nasir is such a loser."

He casually made his way onto the sidewalk, first checking to make sure no one saw him leaving Nasir's backyard. "All's clear."

As he walked by his house, which was now a hellish nightmare of flames and falling debris, he called one of his friends and gushed about the tragedy of his neighbor's life. "I just can't believe someone would let their life fall apart like that," he gossiped, incredulous to the destruction of his own home in the background.

Carter continued his trek down the sidewalk, only glancing for a second at his now fiery home. "Ahh, it's not that serious."

"What's not that serious?" his friend asked him over the phone.

"Ah nothing, just a tiny flare-up. No big deal. So yeah, like I was saying, Nasir tries way too hard to make it seem like he's got it all together, but deep down, he's a total mess."

Carter's neighbors began pooling into the street, looking in horror at his burning house.

"Oh my God, Carter!" his neighbor Shakema ran up to him. "Your house! Your house! Have you called the fire—"

"Relax, relax. Nothing to worry about. Everything is fine."

In a state of total confusion, Shakema watched as he continued striding down the sidewalk. "What? Aren't you gonna do something? Your house is on fire!"

"Calm down. It's not that serious. Now just go on and mind your business, okay?"

As he turned around and continued walking, Shakema dialed 911, her hands trembling. Then she ran back toward the crowd of neighbors in the street.

"What was that about?" his friend asked, having heard Shakema over the phone.

"Oh, nothing. Just some nosy neighbors who need to mind their own business," Carter responded loudly enough for others to hear as he looked back in Shakema's direction. "Seriously, some people need to get a life."

Screams rang out as a gust of wind carried embers from Carter's house onto the trees behind his house. The flames quickly spread across the trees and within minutes they were completely engulfed. The burning trees snapped and landed onto two other houses. The neighbors that had gathered in the street made desperate attempts to spray water onto all three houses with water hoses. Other families joined in their efforts and formed an assembly line to transport buckets of water to the houses until the firetrucks arrived.

Meanwhile, Carter continued his casual stroll, his mind and conversation still focused on Nasir's "tragic" life.

"Just promise me you'll never let me end up like Nasir, man. I don't ever want to be *that* ridiculous."

Hypocrite! First remove the plank from your own eye, and then you will see clearly to remove the speck from your brother's eye.

Matthew 7:5

Knock Out

*R*ats! He keeps picking up his phone. Here we go again. I look around at my team and give an affirmative nod.

"He's coming with *me*."

Fear quickly snatched Matt's focus out of our hands and ran back to her group like a tiny mouse. She dove into the middle of their huddle, foolishly thinking that this maneuver would shield her.

"Let's go!" I commanded, motioning for my team to attack Fear.

My team sprang into action at my command. We charged toward the huddle, our eyes set intently on Fear in the middle. One by one, we picked up Confusion, Pain, Worry, and Stress. We circled around Fear, who was still clutching Matt's focus with all her might.

"He's mine," Fear hissed. "I'm not letting go of him!"

From behind us at least ten different distractions swarmed us like bees. They drove their sharp teeth into each of us with strategic speed. In the time it took us to tear them off us, the huddle that had covered Fear had regrouped, and marched toward us with ferocity.

"Push back—now!" I commanded, and we sliced our way through this terrible crowd. "Matt's still praying, team. We've got to *push*; we can't let him stop."

We wildly threw punch after punch. To my left I saw Confusion weaving and bobbing all over the place, zigzagging, faking lefts and rights like no other. Stress was beginning to wrap itself tightly around one of my team members like a snake, inching higher and higher, aiming toward their head. To my right Lust quickly kept appearing and disappearing in different spots around the rink, vanishing each time we tried to catch her. Only Pain and Worry were left protecting Fear. But now the distractions were coming back, and boy did they bite hard. Fully serving their purpose, the distractions kept us from advancing every time we had to stop and fight them off us.

This fight was getting tough. I looked down and saw Matt walking out of his prayer closet, dialing a number in his phone.

No!

"Finish them!" I yelled, my voice reflecting the urgency rising in me once I saw that Matt's prayers had ceased. "Finish. Them. *Now!*"

And with that, we pushed back with an onslaught of Biblical proportions. We pushed and pushed and pushed. I was determined not to stop until Fear's neck was in both of my hands.

Before I knew it, Fear was being dropped at my feet. She had been completely butchered. Still holding onto Matt's focus with all her might, she cowered over it in a fetal position, pitifully whimpering with—you guessed it—fear.

"No, please don't. I've been with him for so long."

"Enough with the theatrics, cupcake, cough it up."

I wrestled it away from her and covered it with my wings. Taking Matt's focus back to my camp, I began undoing the damage done during the fight for it. I finally had another chance to peek down below. Matt was in the shower now, having a full-on worship concert. *Whew!* Showers make great prayer closets too.

"Good fight today, team," I said when we gathered around back at home base. "We had a couple close calls, but we pushed through each time. I don't know about you, but I sure wanna toss Matt's phone out the window after today."

Crossroads

"**G**o right, my dude. Right!"

I was playing the role of a personal cheerleader at this point. My friend down below began inching toward the left.

Please don't let me have a front-row seat to an epic fail. Please, not today, God.

When you see someone you've been rooting for about to lose, it's hard. My friend has been in this same place for years, and at any second he could take a turn for the worse and never come back. I've seen it happen a million times before. I began to pace.

"*C'mon* man. Come *on*. I've been with you since day one; it can't end like this!"

My marching orders were to stay put, which was why I was so restless. I was used to stepping in for my friend at the ninth hour. But I couldn't this time. I wasn't allowed to step in anymore. It was all between him and God now, so there was nothing more I could do.

"*Please, please* don't take another step that way. *Please!*"

The next thing I knew, my friend was running toward the right. He moved so fast that he was already well on his way before I realized what was happening. Thank God—literally.

My friends crowded around me and joined in on the celebration, cheering and shouting. I turned around. "Yes, he made it! Party time!"

Likewise, I say to you, there is joy in the presence of the angels of God over one sinner who repents.

Luke 15:10

Conclusion

"**S**o, what've you got for me?" my boss asked as our meeting began.

"A lot," I answered, going through all 187 pages with Him. "From start to finish, the goal was to show everyone how much You love us and also illustrate what we do with Your love, plus a little bit of an angelic perspective too. This will likely help us turn the mirror on ourselves, especially regarding how we treat You at times. Hopefully all this makes us ask ourselves the important questions:

Am I really down to ride?

Is there a bomb of unforgiveness strapped to my chest?

Do I have scoliosis now because I've tried to carry everything by myself?

Am I a Jovan, enjoying my plans, or a Niecy enjoying Your presence?"

"Those are some great questions. They really get to the heart of the matter. But what if they ask these questions and still don't get the message?"

I was relieved He asked. "That's exactly what I stopped by to ask You. I've been praying and fasting about all this, and what I really need is Your blessing. None of this matters if Your Hand isn't in it."

"You're right about that. Thank you for taking care of business—my business."

"Of course. It's been an honor." I stood up to go begin my day. "I'm so blessed to know that You used me for this amaz—"

"Now, let's talk about your next book," He said, *way* too nonchalantly in my opinion. "I definitely want a chapter titled *Encore*, referring to people who get up to leave before the grand finale. You know, kinda just like you were about to do."

"Excuse me? My *next* book?"

"You *are* down to ride, aren't you?"

Well played, Boss Man. I see what You did right there.

"But I thought I was done. I may have stopped and started over and over again, but I did finish it. Just like you wanted."

"Right. And I've blessed you for doing that. You'll see. But at what point did I say this would be the only book you would write?"

"You didn't, but ..."

He smiled. "You thought you were one and done, huh?"

"Yeah, I guess so." I was somewhat embarrassed. I really had to stop putting words in His mouth.

"I agree, we're definitely gonna work on that," He responded in regards to my last thought. "But you've gotten a lot better. In fact, you're actually going to write about exactly that. I can see the title now: *What I Thought vs What God Said*. It's got a nice ring to it, don't ya think?"

With a smile I sat back down and reopened my journal to take notes from our meeting. Of course God isn't done with me. Of course He's always got something up ahead that He's been planning, just when I think I'm done. And of course I don't mind doing His bidding, because I trust that it will keep getting better. How could I possibly say no? He promised me that my latter would be greater than my former, so it's a win-win!

I wrote a short phrase at the top of my journal entry for the day:

LATTER > FORMER

God is pretty awesome, after all. He certainly keeps His promises. We just gotta be sure to keep our promises to Him.

About the Author

Donna Robinson is a devoted follower of Christ and human rights activist. Having lived and worked in countries in the Middle East and sub-Saharan Africa, Donna is committed to ending the scourge of modern-day slavery and other human rights abuses through the power of God.

Connect with **Relatable God** online:

Instagram: @relatablegod

Twitter: @relatablegod_

YouTube: @relatablegod

Facebook: @relatablegod

CPSIA information can be obtained
at www.ICGtesting.com
Printed in the USA
BVHW041636150421
605035BV00008B/449

9 780578 799209